A RELUCTANT

PANTHEISM

Other books by Walt McLaughlin:

Cultivating the Wildness Within
(essays)

The Impossible Cosmos
A Year of Amateur Astronomy and Big Questions
(science, narrative)

The Unexpected Trail
Taking on the 100 Mile Wilderness
(narrative)

Forest under my Fingernails
Reflections and Encounters on the Long Trail
(narrative)

The Allure of Deep Woods
Backpacking the Northville-Placid Trail
(narrative)

Arguing with the Wind
A Journey into the Alaskan Wilderness
(narrative)

Backcountry Excursions
Venturing into the Wild Regions of the Northeast
(short narratives)

Loon Wisdom
Sounding the Depths of Wildness
(essays and short narratives)

Nature and Existence
(philosophical essays)

A Hungry Happiness
(poetry)

A RELUCTANT PANTHEISM

Discovering the Divine in Nature

by

Walt McLaughlin

Wood Thrush Books

The cover image of a fossil at Fisk Quarry was
taken by Walt McLaughlin

Published by Wood Thrush Books
            27 Maple Grove Estates
            Swanton, Vermont 05488

ISBN 978-0-9903343-6-1

Acknowledgements

It is impossible to name all those who have helped me better understand the relationship between God, man and nature, or who have assisted me in my spiritual journey, but I feel compelled to recognize a few of the major players. My parents, Margaret & G. James McLaughlin, were the earliest influences, of course. My mother, a true Christian, first got me thinking about God and the world at large. My father showed me a book called *The Five Great Philosophies of Life* when I was very young, thus opening another door. A Catholic priest, Reverend John M. Fulcher, took the time to sit down and discuss religious and philosophical matters with me on several occasions at a critical point in my teenage years, and a philosophy professor, Dr. Donald Borchert, carried on this rather difficult task when I was in college. My college roommate and good friend, David Kaufman, was both a sounding board and the voice of reason in countless philosophical discussions, helping me work out the initial framework of my worldview.

During my rambling years, fellow aspiring writers Peter Yates Hodshon and Mark Katzman introduced me to all sorts of ideas, and encouraged me to keep writing and thinking no matter what. As a young bookseller in Burlington, Vermont, I was surrounded by many dynamic minds, but three in particular stand out: Andrew Bernardin, Michael Jewell, and Richard Donnelly. Andrew introduced me to Zen Buddhism early on. Later he challenged my theology with hard science as his own worldview evolved. Michael opened the world of Indian thought to me. He and I have contrasted and compared our respective spiritual journeys on many occasions since then. Richard, who once flirted with Nihilism but now sees the world in a more practical light, has always found the humor in my darkest philosophical ruminations. I lean heavily on him to this day.

In later years, I have been blessed with many literary friends who embrace wild nature without shrugging off the deepest human concerns: Walt Franklin, Benjamin Green, Rob Faivre, Howard Nelson, t. kilgore splake, Clarence Wolfshohl, and Scott King to name a few. I can't begin to thank them all for helping me cultivate my ideas and express them more effectively.

During the writing of this book, two literary friends have been particularly helpful: Frederick Moe and William Weiss. Fred has cheered on my spiritual development since the mid 90s. He encouraged me to see this project through even when I had serious doubts about it. Bill played a more direct role, fleshing out Taoism for me, opening my mind to other ways of seeing the world, and supplying a steady stream of suggested readings during the eleventh hour of this project. I am deeply indebted to him.

Last but not least, there is my life partner, Judy Ashley, who has provided emotional support during the past three decades of my philosophical wandering. Without her, I doubt I would have had the courage to continue traveling this long and twisting path, much less write about it. To her I owe more than I can say.

Contents

Prologue: Chazy Reef 11

1   Godtalk 16
2   The Ultimate Question . . 26
3   Reason and Revelation . . 33
4   Spiritual Wandering . . 44
5   The Cult of Alders . . 54
6   God's Nature . . . 61
7   Natural Theology . . . 69
8   Belief and Unbelief . . 78
9   The Divine Cosmos . . 85
10   God and Wildness . . . 94
11   The Pantheistic Worldview . 103
12   The Grand Scheme of Things . 109
13   A Reluctant Pantheism . . 115

Epilogue: Eternal Renewal . . . 123

Notes 128

Most people with whom I talk, men and women
even of some originality and genius,
have their scheme of the universe all cut and dried...
dry enough to burn.

– Henry David Thoreau

A RELUCTANT
PANTHEISM

Prologue: Chazy Reef

Isle La Motte in northern Vermont is the last place in the world one would expect to find the fossil remnants of an ancient coral reef, but there it is. After procrastinating for nearly a decade, I am finally making a pilgrimage to it. I want to see with my own eyes what I've come to accept as a matter of fact: that life forms have evolved over hundreds of millions of years on this planet. I pull my car over to the side of the road, close to a sign marking the trail to Fisk Quarry. My wife Judy waits patiently in the car. She knows that I'm a man on a mission so she's giving me the room I need to completely immerse myself in the great mysteries of time and stone. Afterward I'll be in a better frame of mind to resume our leisurely autumnal drive.

I set forth down the trail at a brisk pace. Matika, my long-haired German shepherd, is right on my heels. She is completely in the moment, taking in the sights, sounds and smells all around us – especially the smells. I am not as much in the present. Unlike my animal companion, I am deep into abstractions, only vaguely aware of my immediate surroundings. I am more interested in what this place once was than what it is right now.

A few minutes down the trail, the abandoned quarry comes into view. Fisk Quarry, where a unique limestone called "black marble" was cut then hauled away for public buildings back in the 19th century, is now one of two national landmark sites overseen by the Isle La Motte Preservation Trust. The other is the Goodsell Ridge Preserve a few miles away. Both are part of a geological formation called Chazy Reef that dates back 480 million years. The remnants of this reef stretch from Quebec to Tennessee. Most of it is now buried well beneath the surface of the earth. Only a few sections are exposed. The lower half of a twelve-square-mile island in Lake Champlain called Isle La Motte is one of the few places where one can readily see this reef. Hard to believe that it was once located where Africa is today, that the earth's tectonic plates have shifted that far over time. Then again, a lot of things can happen in half a billion years.

While circumnavigating the quarry, I notice bizarre shapes in the black and grey rock underfoot. I have never seen anything quite like them before. Bryozoa and other primordial life forms built this reef. Coral came later, then a host of ancient marine creatures inhabited it: cephalopods, brachiopods, trilobites, and so on. What I am seeing now are the vague outlines of those creatures set in stone. There are more of them than I can count. I amble across the storied rock in a daze. When finally I reach the top of the quarry, I find the distinctive swirls of large gastropods – the distant ancestors of modern snails. I kneel down for a closer look.

Seeing is believing, they say, but I find it difficult to comprehend what my eyes are telling me.

Are these really the fossils of creatures that lived several hundred million years ago? They spread before me in all directions. Skeptic that I am, I reach down and touch them, one right after another. Then I pull out my camera and snap dozens of pictures in order to assure myself later that these fossils really do exist, that this wasn't just a dream.

Caw, caw! A murder of crows flies by. I hear the chips and calls of robins, sparrows and other familiar birds as well. I raise my eyes to the sun burning through a thin film of cloud cover and feel its heat on my face. A balmy, October breeze caresses my brow. Matika smiles that great big canine smile of hers as she looks around. A frog croaks from the placid water that has filled the quarry. The leaves still clinging to the trees around me are green, gold and burnt orange. While fingering the subtle contours of a fossilized gastropod, I try to sync the deep past with the present. It's no use. There isn't enough grey matter between my ears to do so. Too much time has passed; too much change has transpired. I am astonished.

Then I see it. I see in the ghostly apparitions at my fingertips the whorl of flowers, hurricanes and spiral galaxies. I see patterns manifesting themselves at all levels, from the smallest, subatomic particles to the grand structure of the universe as a whole. I see order where there should be only chaos. Is this the hand of God in the world? What else can it be? Knowing that the universe I inhabit has not been here forever, what other conclusion can I draw?

The swirl of gastropods and galaxies is unmistakable. It is existence turning back onto itself, taking shape out of formlessness. It is nothing less than nature organizing. In moments like this, the yawning chasm between mathematics and mysticism suddenly vanishes, and I understand on some level of consciousness how everything connects. I see with my mind's eye how one has become many while retaining its oneness. And this seeing, this wordless comprehension of the real is a profound experience – a deeply *religious* experience in the truest sense of the word.

I do not consider myself a pious man. I am no saint, shaman, or guru by any stretch of the imagination. I abandoned organized religion a long time ago, and after hearing my opinions on theological matters, most people would call me a secular thinker. Yet I am convinced that there is more to the universe than meets the eye, that nature is driven by forces we are only beginning to fathom. And it is reasonable, I think, to assume that these forces emanate from a single source. That is precisely what the word "God" is all about, although there are other words for it to be sure.

A family of four comes along while I am kneeling down contemplating spirals and spirituality. The parents bring the embedded fossils to the attention of their two children, trying to explain what is so clearly written in stone. It's no use. Such concepts are lost on 5- and 7-year olds. Might as well try to explain it all to my dog, Matika. Both dogs and young children live too much in the present to entertain such abstractions. Unlike my dog, though, children can at least ape their parents, verbalizing some semblance of understanding. But the knowing is not there. The knowing comes from deep within, once one has lived long enough and gathered enough information about the world to tell the difference between reality and mere appearances. Can this also be said about humanity as a whole? Is human history nothing more than our gradual coming of age? Are those of us living today more knowing than the first humans? Some people would be inclined to say yes. Others would vehemently disagree.

While following the trail, slowly working my way back to the car, I consider how much I know about the world compared to what I don't know. In many ways, I'm no wiser than my dog. Like her, I am a living, breathing animal with a host of physical needs and desires that take me away from my abstractions time and time again. Is this a bad thing? No, it is good to live in one's body and fully engage the world that way. On the other hand, abstract thinking is what I, *Homo sapiens*, do best. So I don't ignore my abstractions when they come calling. In fact, I have spent a great deal of time and energy during the past forty-odd years cultivating them. In a round about way, they draw me closer to God.

1. Godtalk

We live in the natural world – a world of fire and ice, earth and water. The wind blows, rocking skyscrapers and other manmade structures where so many of us sit and stare at computers. Microbes are everywhere, infesting everything. They make up a significant portion of the bodies that we call our own. We share this world with all kinds of flora and fauna that are caught in an endless cycle of birth and death, growth and decay, consuming each other in a frenzy of activity that astounds us whenever we take the time to really think about it. Like them, we eat and drink our way through the days, leaving excrement and urine in our wake. Like them, we are born and eventually die.

Overhead on a clear night, when the sun is no longer bleaching out the sky, we see a large orb that we call the moon along with countless smaller specs of twinkling light. Upon close inspection, the moon appears to have texture, as do a few of those other specs of light – the ones that we call planets. They are distant worlds similar to our own in some ways yet completely alien in others. Most of the remaining specs of light in the night sky are stars like our sun. Some of those specs are clouds of gas where stars are formed. Some are great cities of stars called galaxies, so far away that a flash of light from one of them takes millions of years to reach us, sometimes billions. Clearly, our world is only one of many.

These are the simple facts that we have learned over the past few hundred years. It is pointless to deny any of it. Yet the vast majority of us go about our daily affairs as if all this is irrelevant, as if there are more important things to think about than the fundamentals of existence. Many of us insulate ourselves from such thoughts with belief systems that we have inherited from our parents. Some cultivate more materialistic worldviews that focus upon self-gratification with little regard for anything else. A few embrace esoteric philosophies and religions that explain everything. There is no limit it seems to how far we are willing to go to avoid thinking about these simple facts. What is it about them that we find so terrifying?

Death is the big bugaboo, of course. Unlike other animals, we are highly cognizant creatures acutely aware of our own mortality. And when we think about our eventual demise, all kinds of questions arise – questions to which there are no simple answers. Foremost among those questions is this: Why do we exist at all? The meaning of our existence, or the lack thereof, haunts us. We can't escape it.

It appears that we are alone in this. Even among our closest relatives, the other primates, we seem to be the only ones that contemplate death. As the archeologist Grahame Clark pointed out in his book, *Space, Time and Man*, "Among the non-human primates dead animals have no meaning." There are no burial rituals indicating that they do, anyhow. Such rituals appear in our own archeological record over 30,000 years ago. Those rituals mark a distinctive break with our primal, non-reflective past.

"When people first began to ask themselves the meaning of death," Clark observed, "They posed a question to which priests and philosophers and not least their audiences have been addressing themselves ever since." And so it is. Religion and philosophy were born in those first burial rituals. Those rituals prove that our distant ancestors had gained an acute awareness of time – past, present, and future – and were looking for their place in it. They groped for meaning the same way that we grope for it today, resolving the matter the best way they could before getting on with life. But meaning is not easily resolved.

We think therefore we question the meaning of existence – not just the meaning of our own existence, the meaning of everything, of the universe at large. There has to be some point to it all. The entire universe could be nothing more than a random series of events, but that doesn't seem likely. Our thoughts alone, and the biological mechanisms that allow them, seem to undercut that possibility. How could a creature as sophisticated as a human being emerge from nature by sheer accident? Surely some external force must have created us, along with the order of things that is so apparent in the natural world. Either that or there are fundamental laws built into nature that are unchanging and eternal.

This questioning process is as old as humanity itself. We are questioning animals by nature – the only ones that appear to do so. This process makes us religious/philosophical animals, simply because every question begs an answer. That no definitive answers are forthcoming does not change the fact that questions have been asked. Even if one immediately dismisses them, the questions have still been asked.

Why did we come to be? This most vexing question leads to a multitude of other related questions. Why is there something instead of nothing? Where do the laws of physics come from? Why it the universe the way it is? We have accumulated a mountain of natural facts through the millennia, thanks to science, but the nature of nature itself remains beyond our grasp. The world in which we live – the natural world – remains shrouded in mystery. And, as Ursula Goodenough points out in her book, *The Sacred Depths of Nature*, "The word God is often used to name this mystery." Not everyone is comfortable with that word, but the mystery it represents has been with us for a long, long time.

As the great ice sheets that covered much of our planet receded twelve thousand years ago, the first human societies came into being. In these societies, people lived close to the earth. To them the world was full of spirits both helpful and hurtful. We moderns call this basic belief system Animism, even though most of its practitioners wouldn't have considered their spirit stories any kind of system at all. They didn't think that way. Their stories were simply the answers they created to address the most pointed questions about how things are and how they came to be. Their stories were the means by which people could live their lives in the face of harsh, unfathomable realities. And it was all perfectly natural. "The man of the archaic societies tends to live as much as possible *in* the sacred," wrote Mircea Eliade in *The Sacred and the Profane*. What we moderns call religious sentiment permeated every aspect of their lives, that is. There was no delineation back then between the worldly and the otherworldly. That came later.

As civilizations developed in river valleys and elsewhere, these animistic belief systems morphed into polytheistic religions. In other words, the spirits became gods, and a dominant creator god usually emerged from the pack. The Babylonian civilization had Marduk for example. Marduk was a powerful sun god who created all of humanity. The Hindus had Brahma; the Egyptians had Ra. Centuries later, the Greeks had Zeus. The Romans had Jupiter. Each was a great god among equals.

What does all this indicate? Only that humankind as a whole has a powerful urge to fill in the gaps, to make sense of the world, to make known the unknown somehow. As the centuries went by, our gods became more numerous and elaborate. Civilizations have come and gone, but the desire to answer the most fundamental questions, to resolve the great mysteries of nature, has stayed with us. This desire defines us. It is practically built into our DNA. *Homo sapiens* is the animal in search of the divine.

The gods are angry. The gods are compassionate. They can be crafty, jealous, vindictive, playful, ruthless, loving, and much more. They exhibit the full range of emotions, just like us. That's because they *are* us. The gods are mirror images of us. In the deliberate attempts of our ancestors to understand the world, especially the most mysterious aspects of it, they projected human qualities upon the creative and destructive forces of nature. In other words, their gods were *anthropomorphic*, and rightly so. After all, it is hard to imagine a god that isn't something like us. There is, of course, the imposing reality of that massive grey matter between our ears – what clearly distinguishes us from all other animals. Surely the gods are as cognizant and self-aware as we are. Or so our ancestors reasoned. And if we are honest with ourselves, we must admit that we moderns would have reasoned the same way they did if we had lived several thousand years ago. In fact, some of us still think this way today.

Not only are the gods like us, the world itself exists for our benefit. We occupy the center stage. In other words, our worldviews tend to be *anthropocentric*. Our ancestors assumed that we are the main actors in the drama being played out in the universe, that human history is the crux of all natural history. Our ancestors took the sky at face value. The stars revolve around our world, as do the sun and the moon. And who are the most important players in this world? Surely not fish, insects, birds, or furry creatures no matter how big or ferocious they might be. No, we are the dominant ones. So any grand scheme put into place by the gods must revolve around us, certainly.

In hindsight it is easy for us moderns to look upon the ancients with condescending eyes. The earth-centered universe is long gone. We now know for a fact that our planet is only one of many revolving around the sun. We also know that the sun is but one of a hundred billion stars in a galaxy that we call the

Milky Way, and that there are hundreds of billions of galaxies like our own scattered across a universe so large that it is unfathomable. We know all this thanks to our reasoning abilities, and the long, arduous accumulation of scientific facts. Because of these facts, it is difficult nowadays to still believe that humankind has a significant role in the drama being played out in the cosmos. It's even more difficult to conceptualize the divine once the twin crutches of anthropomorphism and anthropocentrism have been taken away.

Godtalk. Is it really necessary? Some people say good riddance to the gods. Some say that the divine itself is a fantasy, that reason has replaced any need for it. Such people pride themselves on being utterly rational thinkers, putting their faith in science not the mumbo-jumbo of high priests, shamans or witch doctors. Nature operates according to laws that can be scientifically verified, they say. All across the universe, both matter and energy adhere to the same basic laws of physics, they assure us. This is true, certainly, but it doesn't explain where those laws came from.

The more answers that science gives us regarding nature, the more questions arise. It's a vicious circle. We go round and round proving this and disproving that until finally we are face-to-face with the unknown again. Then what? Then secular or religious, each of us takes a leap of faith. What other choice do we have, really? There is no such thing as a scientific worldview. Science is a process, not a belief system.

"A purely rational man is an abstraction," Mircea Eliade declared, "He is never found in real life. Every human being is made up at once of his conscious activity and his irrational experiences." The key concept here is "irrational experiences." The world and the lives that we live never make perfect sense. Contradictions and paradoxes persist. The absurd arises daily, undercutting the most rational worldview. More to the point, the universe retains its greatest mysteries despite our best efforts to make sense of it.

Some say that the universe doesn't make sense because it's utterly random. In a random universe, things may appear to make sense but they don't really. Nothing makes sense in a universe where the laws of physics are not laws at all, where everything is subject to immediate, serendipitous change. The word "random" is unforgiving. It strips away all cause and effect. In that case, what's the point of clinging to reason? What is logic but a pipedream when a fundamental statement like "if p then q" has no meaning whatsoever?

On the other hand, in a universe that's the least bit organized, one can't help but wonder what that organizing force is. Let me rephrase that. *I* can't help but wonder what that organizing force is. I can't speak for you. Perhaps you are perfectly comfortable living with the absurdity of an organized yet inexplicable universe. Perhaps you don't wonder about how or why it is organized. Or perhaps you have more immediate concerns to think about. All I know is that I can't get away from it.

Godtalk is unavoidable for those of us who feel compelled to get to the root of it all. The ancient Greeks had Logos. The ancient Chinese had Tao. Others since them have given the Absolute a variety of names: One, Idea, Being, etc. Some say Nature is the ultimate reality, making sure to capitalize the "N." The use of capital letters is the dead giveaway. The absolute becomes the Absolute the moment we load it with meaning. Philosophers tend to shy away from the word "God" in their rational arguments, but they too engage in godtalk. Even the most secular-thinking cosmologists engage in it, although they may avoid creating any sort of proper noun for the ultimate reality about which they speculate. The only way to avoid godtalk is to avoid speculating about ultimate reality altogether.

As for me, I have been speculating about ultimate reality for the better part of my life. Because of this habit I call myself a philosopher, but you can call me a mystic if you want. Superficially, the difference between a philosopher and a mystic is that the former uses reason to speculate about ultimate reality while the latter opts for direct encounter. But the philosopher does not rely upon reason alone, nor is the mystic incapable of it. Both are thinking creatures belonging to the same brainy species. Both are animals immersed in their experiences, worldly or otherwise. Although some people may still differentiate between philosophy and mysticism, I stopped doing that a long time ago.

So what exactly is the ultimate reality? What is this thing that we call God? Do we err the moment we start thinking about it as a thing? Do we err the moment we start thinking about it at all? These are but a few of the questions that arise whenever we engage in godtalk. It's a quagmire to be sure. It seems like our minds are not quite up to the task. More often than not, we approach the subject with the best of intentions and end up worshipping false idols. That's because there is no absolute answer to what the Absolute is. How much easier it is to opt out, to short circuit the vicious circle of unknowing and settle for something less. That way we can get on with our lives in some semblance of certainty no matter how unfounded that certainty may be.

Like I said before, I am no saint, shaman or guru by any stretch of the imagination. All I have to offer regarding the divine is a fistful of speculations based upon what I've read, experienced, and thought deeply about. My only credential is that I'm a tireless seeker. I have spent the better part of my life in hot pursuit of ultimate reality, frequently getting lost or sidetracked in the process. I've taken all kinds of detours along the way, and have caught glimpses of the divine only to have it escape me. Deep in wild places where few people tread, I have encountered it the most. But the wild is not limited to those places that we fence off and declare wilderness areas. It's all around us all the time. We live in the natural world despite appearances to the contrary, despite our preoccupations with manmade things. Hence the divine is like ripe fruit that is always ready for the picking. To encounter it, all one has to do is reach out.

2. The Ultimate Question

Before my awakening, I was a good Catholic boy. I went to church with my mother on holy days, confessed my sins, took communion, and sang the hymns. In my early teens, I went to Sunday school and studied the New Testament with a farmer of humble means whose steely blue eyes burned bright with the word of God. Shortly thereafter I purchased a hardcover copy of *The Jerusalem Bible* then took it upon myself to read the entire thing from cover to cover. What I found there was shocking. No one had warned me about the carnage and cruelty that's so pervasive in the Old Testament, or the apparent madness of the prophets, or the errant ways of David and other deeply religious men. It all seemed far removed from my middle class, Midwestern American upbringing and the complexities of the world in the 20th century. Had I been a normal teenager, I would have taken the scriptures at face value and dismissed most of it. But I took it to heart instead.

The Book of Revelation really got to me. As I pored over those prophecies about the end of days, I started seeing the early warning signs of the coming apocalypse all around me, wondering what my role would be when the time came. Books about the apocalypse, cleverly designed to scare folks into embracing fundamentalist Christianity, were easy to come by. I read a few of them but they only heightened my confusion. The disparities between what I found in the Bible and what those books were saying about it were great indeed. So I focused my attention on the sacred text itself and dismissed everything else. At the time it seemed like the best course of action. But that wasn't the smartest thing for a troubled teenager like me to do.

Troubled? No more than most kids growing up in the 60s and 70s I suppose. The social fabric seemed to be coming apart at the seams, there was nothing but war abroad and civil strife at home, and drugs were all too easy to come by. But none of that concerned me. Not really. My trouble was deep within. I didn't know who I was, and the bipolar tendencies that I had inherited from my father made it difficult for me to get a handle on things. So then, like the prophets of old, I found myself on the road to divine inspiration. Either that or madness.

By the summer of '72 I was reading messages in the night stars, seeing ghostly apparitions in misty Ohio cornfields, and writing cryptic hieroglyphs during hypnotic stupors. In other words, my life had taken a bad turn. The madness was winning. Yet a desire to understand, to truly understand the world, still burned white-hot inside me.

It seemed as if all I lacked was direction so I went back to the source. In the middle of a sultry August night, I tugged on all the doors of a nearby church until one opened. I went in, knelt before the altar in darkness, and prayed for guidance. And then, to my own great surprise, I let out a loud, monosyllabic howl: *Why?* The question echoed through the vaults overhead, gradually fading to silence. No answer was forthcoming. Silence. I burst into tears, babbling like a fool about how confusing everything was. I blathered on and on, talking to God, but God did not answer. Only silence.

When my folks asked me where I'd been that night, I told them the truth. Shortly thereafter I found myself in a hospital psyche ward, face-to-face with a bespectacled, grinning Gestalt psychiatrist. It was a depressing turn of events to say the least. I had spiritual work to do yet here I was drugged, incarcerated, and expected to talk about my feelings. The priest at the local church came to visit me, and for a moment or two I thought he would make everything right. But our brief conversation was a tremendous disappointment. He couldn't help me out of this quagmire. I was on my own. A couple weeks later, I was released from the hospital on the condition that I continue taking the cocktail of drugs that the psychiatrist had prescribed in order to stabilize my mood. I agreed to that stipulation even though it felt like I was somehow compromising myself. I sank deeper into depression during the months that followed. Then one cold day I came up with a solution. I decided to end it all. I hitchhiked to an arboretum half a dozen miles into the wintry countryside. It was closed for the season. There I sat in a Japanese garden dusted with snow, staring at a bunch of sleeping pills that I had poured into my hand. It would be an easy death and no one would find me until spring. That was the plan, anyhow. But a blackbird came along, begging for the food it thought I was holding, and that broke the spell.

Not long afterward, I dumped all my prescription drugs on the psychiatrist's desk while barking with a few choice words at him. With a self-satisfied smile he declared me cured. Then I struck out on my own down the cold, dark tunnel of depression. I stopped going to school. I stopped interacting with people. I lived like a vampire, active at night and asleep most of the day. Eventually I stopped eating. Then it came, completely without warning. The clouds broke open on a frigid February morning and the sun shined so brightly that I couldn't resist it. I ran out the door, dancing barefoot in the snow and basking in sunlight. And that was it – I awakened from the nightmare. I went back inside to warm up and eat something. Then I slowly put my life back together, one piece at a time.

Why? Why is the world the way that it is? How did it come to be? What is it all for? Why am I in it? "We exist within the question of God," the scholar William Barrett recently wrote, echoing the 18th century philosopher Immanuel Kant, "We cannot escape it; it is always there for us, however we may seek to forget or evade it." That question can be posed many different ways, with an emphasis on *how* or *what* instead of *why*, but it all comes down to the same thing. It can be posed spiritually or philosophically, as a religious matter or as a scientific one, in any language imaginable. But once asked, it cannot be taken back.

One could argue that it is precisely this question that separates us from the rest of creation, that asking why is Adam biting into the forbidden fruit, and that our banishment from the blissful ignorance of the Garden of Eden is the direct consequence of it. Asking this question is an awakening to be sure – the distinct mark of self-awareness that we all share. However we frame the question, one thing is clear: the answer lies well beyond us, in a realm so ethereal that even the word "God," however appropriate, seems to fall short of the mark.

Although the tribulation that I underwent as a teenager might seem more psychological than religious, it was not far removed from what other spiritual seekers have experienced throughout the ages. The 16th century Spanish mystic St. John of the Cross had a good term for it. He called this tribulation *the dark night of the soul*. When seekers find no pleasure in God or the world He has created, when it seems to them like they are backsliding spiritually into oblivion, losing all faith either through negligence or sin, the dark night has arrived. "But this trouble that they are taking is quite useless," St. John of the Cross says, "For God is now leading them by another road, which is that of contemplation."

What exactly *is* contemplation? It is neither prayer nor thought, yet it is both. One sits and contemplates the world and one's place in it. One contemplates all existence – life and its meaning. One contemplates God. This began for me when I stopped being a Catholic, a good Christian, or a member of any organized religion. The priest who visited me in the hospital took the time later on to sit down and discuss spiritual matters with me on several occasions. No doubt he must have felt like he had failed to get this stray lamb back into the fold, but our discussions helped me immeasurably at the beginning of my long journey down "another road." With his assistance, I emerged from my tribulation a contemplative philosopher, a spiritual wanderer. And I've been one ever since.

The terrible silence. In the church that night, I shouted my question into the universe, expecting God to answer. I waited for Him to speak to me in a baritone voice emanating from a burning bush or something like that. But all I got was silence. I felt cheated. I felt abandoned. What had I done wrong? Silence... nothing but silence... and my own pathetic attempts to conjure up some semblance of God's voice from nothingness. Yet there was a limit to my madness even at the height of this confusion. I talked to God but, no, God did not talk back. All I got for my trouble was that devastating silence.

On many occasions during the past forty years, while wandering in wild places far removed the hustle and bustle of human society, I have posed that same question to the universe. I have posed it in many different ways. Sometimes I have posed it with utterances. Other times I have posed it with a wordless longing from deep within. Always the same response; always that profound silence. But that's okay. Now I understand that silence is the only response there can be to the ultimate question.

Although most people don't think of Henry David Thoreau as a spiritual seeker, it's apparent to me that his woods wanderings led to thoughts and feelings similar to my own. No doubt he knew well the deep silence of wild places, and heard what I hear in it. "The longest silence is the most pertinent question most pertinently put," Thoreau wrote in his journals, "Emphatically silent. The most important question, whose answers concern us more than any, are never put in any other way." Amen to that, brother.

Emphatically silent, yes. But we keep asking the ultimate question anyway. I believe it is our nature to do so. I believe that if the day ever comes when we stop asking that question, when we are convinced that we have the answer to it once and for all, our humanity will vanish. Then we will be self-made gods that the arrogant among us pretend to be, or something much worse. But how likely is that? Not likely at all, really. As long as there's a place wild enough for restless souls like mine to wander and wonder, the ultimate question will be asked. Some of us will never stop asking it. After all, the universe is vast, and our pursuit of the divine is just beginning.

3. Reason and Revelation

What is the proper ground in which to cultivate a worldview: reason or revelation? All religion and philosophy comes down to this, to a fundamental assumption about the best source of knowledge. To secular minds, the choice is clear. Reason is the only way to go. Everything else is wild speculation arising from mythology, superstition, or worse. To strictly religious minds, divine revelation is the only source of truth, and reason is, at best, just an interpretation of it. At worst, it is hubris – a grotesque perversion of reality by godless people who put too much faith in the grey matter between their ears. Most belief systems are a curious blend of the two. But in the final analysis, either reason or revelation must come out on top. Or so we are led to believe.

In 1974 I went off to a university in the hills of southeast Ohio to study philosophy, rejecting the assumption made by so many people that reason and revelation are mutually exclusive. I went to college to study ideas *and* beliefs, to flesh out the notions I had developed during my own teenage tribulations and somehow make sense of them. If pressed to it, I still would have called myself a Christian back then, even though I found it increasingly more difficult to think of Jesus of Nazareth as the one and only Son of God. In the many arguments that I had with Christian fundamentalists outside the classroom, I became convinced that their "one way" worldview had nothing to do with reality. More to the point, I became deeply suspicious of any belief system that embraces faith while dismissing reason altogether, for I had gone down that rabbit hole in my mid-teens and knew all too well where it led. No, blind faith wasn't for me. Before embracing any belief system whatsoever, I first embraced reason. I was convinced that reason was the only way to keep madness at bay. That much I had learned the hard way.

Like all students of Western philosophy, I studied logic, ethics, the differing worldviews of Plato, Aristotle and the Pre-Socratic thinkers, and the more modern ideas of the Empiricists and Rationalists. Through the writings of Plato, I discovered the ancient Greek sage Socrates, who built his worldview upon a healthy respect for uncertainty and adhered to it even in the face of death. About a well-known politician of his day, Socrates said: "He thinks that he knows something which he does not know, whereas I am quite conscious of my ignorance." That resonated with me.

Yes, I studied all the classic philosophers, but the philosophy classroom wasn't the only place where I learned what other people think. Across campus in the political science department, I studied the more worldly views of thinkers like Karl Marx and Thomas Hobbes. In the English department I was exposed to more immediate and humanistic approaches to life, from Shakespeare to the modernists. The beat poets in particular struck a chord in me. They seemed more honest in their approach to the world than anyone else. Because of a strong interest in strategy and tactics, I flirted with the possibility of a military career and enrolled in the Reserve Officers Training Corps. In that environment I witnessed nationalism firsthand, and encountered the dark thoughts of those who had either seen or participated in the many atrocities committed during the Vietnam War. I was also sexually attracted to hippie chicks and found myself discussing the mind-blowing ways of the cosmos while smoking pot with them and their groovy male counterparts. I lived in the International House for a while, rubbing shoulders with people from non-Western cultures. From them I learned that there are many ways of seeing things. In short, mine was a rich and varied education. But halfway through it, I threw a pair highly polished combat boots down a dormitory hallway in a fit of rage. I was getting nowhere. The more I learned, the less I knew about the things that mattered most.

The first thing I did after that was quit the ROTC program. The military was definitely a dead-end road for this seeker. Then I stopped shaving, hoping that my thoughts would grow as wild as my beard. I finished out my spring classes then enrolled in an intensive summer course in the Old Testament. Dr. Borchert taught that course. He was the philosophy professor who had introduced a dozen different worldviews to me in an ethics class I had taken the previous year. He did so without ever revealing his own worldview. I found his approach to beliefs and ideas quite intriguing. He also had a way of cutting to the heart of things while maintaining a sense of humor

– a rare quality among thinkers. If Dr. Borchert couldn't give the Old Testament to me straight then no one could.

To my surprise, I learned more about my Judeo-Christian roots in Borchert's course than I had during several years of solitary study. Yahweh, the God of Abraham, is also Elohim, which is plural for "El" a generic Semitic word for God. Based upon other Semitic peoples mentioned in The Book of Genesis, biblical scholars surmise that Abraham must have lived in the early part of the second millennium BCE. No one knows when exactly. The Old Testament is fuzzy about dates.

Genesis is one of the first five books of the Old Testament. Together those five books are known as the Pentateuch, which is called the Torah in the Judaic tradition. Moses, the founder of Judaism, is credited with writing the Pentateuch, or Torah, but script analysis suggests that it was probably written no earlier than the 10th Century BCE. That places it several hundred years after Moses' death. No matter. Yahweh revealed Himself to Moses on Mount Sinai and that's what kicked off the three great monotheistic religions: Judaism, Christianity and eventually Islam. Through Moses came the Ten Commandments and the covenant between God and the Israelites. It was a definitive break with polytheism. Yahweh revealed Himself to Moses as the one and only God. All other gods are false gods, period.

What good are all these historic details? They flesh out the Old Testament, making real what could otherwise be dismissed as myth. These details weighed heavily on my mind that summer because they placed my Judeo-Christian upbringing in historical context. God had developed *over time*, gradually transforming into the one that I had worshipped as a Catholic. Did any of this help me better understand what I had undergone in my mid-teens? Not really. But it did show the power of revelation, and made me think twice before putting my faith in any philosophy or religion without first giving it a long, hard look.

With a few essentials stuffed into an old Boy Scout rucksack, I stuck out my thumb late in the summer of '76 once the Old Testament course was over. I hitchhiked to British Columbia and back, hoping for a glimpse of the Absolute however it might manifest itself. I was not disappointed. After a couple weeks on the road, I landed on the shoulder of Mt. Baker in the North Cascade Mountains of Washington State. Bright sunlight illuminated the wild landscape all around me as I stood on that snow-covered ridge, looking around. It was nothing short of an encounter with the divine. In that moment I knew deep within that what I had been seeking was right here in the wild, forested landscape sprawling before me in all directions. Without a word being uttered, without the slightest hint of the supernatural, God *revealed* Himself to me. I was certain of it. Now all I had to do was make sense of that revelation. All I had to do was go back home and *reason* my way through it. How hard could that be?

A remarkable shift in human consciousness occurred in the Greek city-states during the 6th Century BCE. A Milesian merchant named Thales looked to the night sky and speculated about what he saw there, applying some of the abstract ideas that he had picked up during his travels to Egypt and elsewhere. His student Anaximander took this line of thought a step further, ultimately writing a book, *On the Nature of Things*, which some scholars consider the first work of natural philosophy. In it, the gods have no place. Anaximenes came along about the same time, seeing the world in terms of natural elements, namely air and its variant forms as earth, water and fire. Elsewhere in Greece, Xenophanes envisioned God as the changeless source of all change in the universe. Heraclitus looked at the world and saw everything in flux. Pythagoras took a more mathematical approach. All these Greek thinkers sought to better understand the world as *Logos* – the natural order of things, a rational force from which all other things emerged. In the following century, Plato would envision God as a Self-mover by which all other things were moved. Aristotle would define God as an Unmoved Mover, standing apart from creation. None of this had anything to do with the capricious gods of Olympus, their tempers, quarrels or vanities.

Greece wasn't the only country where a shift in human consciousness was taking place. In his book *The Marvellous Century*, the historian George Woodcock argues that this shift was universal. "Everywhere in the sixth century the old polytheistic and anthropomorphic attitudes were thus being criticized by thinkers who looked at their world directly," he wrote. A quick survey of what was going on elsewhere in the world reinforces Woodcock's thesis.

In Persia, right next door to Greece, a religious philosopher named Zoroaster had reduced the multitude of Persian gods to two distinct forces, one progressive and the other destructive, overseen by Ahura Mazda, the one God. While no one knows for certain exactly when Zoroaster lived, the ancient Greek historian Herodotus places him in Achaemenian age – a time of great change in Persia. No doubt Zoroastrianism influenced both Greek and Judaic thinkers – the latter subjected to Persian culture when they were part of the Achaemenian Empire. Nowadays the fusion of monotheism with the dualistic concept of good and evil is commonplace, but that wasn't the case 2,500 years ago. Back then it was a revolutionary new way of looking at things.

In the east, Indian philosophy was emerging from a sacred Sanskrit text called *The Vedas*, dating back as far as 4000 BCE. Around the 6th Century BCE, Vedic literature reached its climax with the completion of *The Upanishads*. "Direct experience is the foundation of Indian philosophy,' Pandit Rajmani Tigunait wrote in his book, *Seven Systems of Indian Philosophy*, "But reason and logic are the chief tools that enable the system to grow and develop." This is clearly evident in even a cursory reading of *The Upanishads*. Reason and revelation do not appear to be at odds with each other in eastern minds as they are in western. "*The Upanishads* unanimously maintain the existence of an all-pervasive Reality, called Brahman or Atman," Tigunait asserts. The Hindu version of the divine evolved from polytheistic and anthropomorphic worldviews to a more abstract interpretation of things similar to what the ancient Greeks were thinking at roughly the same time. There is a possibility, of course, that East and West influenced each other through trade and conquest. Then again, it could be that the human mind was simply ready by the 6th century BCE for this big change. Perhaps the time had simply come for humankind to take the next step in its spiritual evolution.

Siddartha Gautama, who also happened to live in India during the 5th or 6th Centuries BCE, was not a big one for delving into abstract metaphysical discussions about God, existence, or the soul. He called these problems *avyaktani*, which is to say indescribable, and focused instead upon the problem of suffering. He founded his religion, Buddhism, on the Four Noble Truths: that suffering exists, that it is caused, that it can be ceased, and that there is a means by which one can cease it. In a sense, Gautama's religion was the first pragmatic one, designed to address the problems apparent in the here and now. But Buddhism is not completely devoid of abstract ideas. The world is subject to universal change, according to the Buddhist way of seeing things. That's a pretty heavy concept. Ideas don't get any more abstract than that.

Farther east, the Hundred Schools of Thought were taking shape in China. Among these, two sages in particular rose to prominence: Confucius and Lao Tzu. Both of these thinkers used reason to better understand the world, although they did so in completely different ways. Confucius emphasized right living, and his worldview focused more on the social and political concerns of the day. Lao Tzu was considerably more abstract by comparison, much more concerned with The Way, or Tao as it is called, than moral or socio-political matters.

Lao Tzu is considered the author of the *Tao Te Ching*, which is the sacred text of Taoism. In it he articulates a Quietist worldview that sees the Tao as an unchanging unity beneath a constantly changing multitude of things. "Such is the scope of the All-pervading Power that it alone can act through the Way," Lao Tzu wrote. "There was something formless yet complete, that existed before heaven and earth," he added. Though it would never occur to a Chinese sage to use a word as mundane as "God," it is clear that the *Tao Te Ching* is about the Absolute and our relationship to it. "Tao gave birth to the One," Lao Tzu said, and it wouldn't have been hard to find an ancient Greek or Indian philosopher to agree with that.

No doubt about it, reason was alive and well in the 6th Century BCE, manifesting itself in many different ways. People everywhere were beginning to think very abstractly about the world in which they lived. Just as the spirits had once yielded to the gods, the gods were now yielding to entirely new worldviews – ones that were as different from each other as they were from past beliefs. Reason infiltrated religion and philosophy came into being. And even though many tried, like the Ch'in emperor who buried alive hundreds of scholars, and the Greeks who served Socrates a cup of hemlock to drink, it was a trend that would prove to be impossible to stop.

Fresh from a month-long tramp out west, I settled back into my studies to finish out my formal education. I took a course in the philosophy of religion and came upon two theologians who made me see things in an entirely different light. One was Jewish; the other was Christian.

Paul Tillich, who grew up Lutheran, wrote a slender book called *Dynamics of Faith*, in which he addressed *ultimate concern* – that which concerns us the most. Ultimate concern is the essence of any given belief system. "If faith is understood as being ultimately concerned," he wrote, "Doubt is a necessary element in it. It is a consequence of the risk of faith." Of course! This is such a simple truth that it's easy to miss. And it smacks of Socratic uncertainty. "Is there a courage which can conquer the anxiety of meaningless and doubt?" Tillich asked in a later work, *The Courage to Be*. "The answer," he went on to say, "Must accept, as its precondition, the state of meaninglessness." And there it was, the essence of every belief system ever invented by humankind boiled down to an existential statement of fact. I couldn't refute it.

Martin Buber, a Hasidic Jew, took a somewhat more mystical approach to the same subject in his book, *I and Thou*. Buber sees God as the Eternal Thou, and our I/You relationship with God is all encompassing. "For those who enter into the absolute relationship, nothing particular retains any importance..." he wrote. Superficially, this relational worldview could be seen as more uplifting than Tillich's, but it harbors the same element of existential despair. "This is the sublime melancholy of our lot that every You must become an It in our world." In other words, the I/You relationship is not a permanent one. Our lives are riddled with moments when we feel completely cut off from others, from the world, even from God. It takes a leap of faith for *I* to recognize another *I*, turning *It* into *You,* and thus initiating a relation. Faith is essential. Doubt is a given. And such relationships must be renewed, over and over again.

That's as far as I got when I graduated from Ohio University with a degree in nothingness. Not exactly what I had set out to do when I first cracked open a college textbook, and definitely not what I had hoped to accomplish after my long tramp out west, but that's the way things go when one strikes out on one's own. There was something in that ecstatic moment on the shoulder of Mt. Baker that gave me hope, but I was no closer to understanding it than I was to understanding the tribulation in my teenage years. Consequently, I walked away from the university feeling educated yet no wiser regarding the most important things. Like Socrates, all I knew for certain was that I knew nothing for certain. In a sense, both reason and revelation had failed me. Either that or I had somehow failed to bring them together. So my quest continued.

4. Spiritual Wandering

Immediately upon graduating from college, I flew to Seattle, Washington to be close to the Cascade Mountains and write a novel based upon my hitchhiking trip out west the previous year. That was my plan, anyhow. Things didn't quite work that way. Writing a novel turned out to be harder than I thought it would be, my few forays into the mountains didn't amount to anything, and the whole affair was cut short by an impulse to rejoin my girlfriend back in Ohio.

Her name was Marge. She was a pretty redhead who only wanted to be a nurse, help other people, and lead a relatively normal life. God only knows what she saw in me, but we were friends as much as we were lovers so it was difficult for either one of us to step away from the relationship. At any rate, I followed her to Boston where she began her career in nursing. I worked in bookstores and continued writing. Time passed. A year and a half later, I talked her into going back out west with me. We stuffed all our worldly possessions into an old Datsun then drove to Arizona where we stayed with friends for a while. After that we went to San Francisco where we hoped to start a new life together.

Marge didn't like San Francisco. We couldn't afford a decent place to live for one thing. When she flopped face down into the hotel bed, breaking into tears, I knew I would have to quickly come up with a plan B. I suggested that we drive north to a small college town in Oregon. Marge liked that idea so off we went. We landed in Eugene, Oregon in the spring of 1980. Shortly after setting up housekeeping in a modest apartment there, we drove into the Cascade Mountains to check things out.

I parked the car at a trailhead on the road to McKenzie Pass, deep in the mountains. Marge stayed in the car while I speed-hiked the two miles of trail leading back to Linton Lake. There I caught the faintest glimmer of the divine. A bald eagle screamed from a high perch across the lake, as if calling me to the wildness beyond. The Three Sisters Wilderness. I marveled at the way it sprawled across the map – a great, green, forested and mountainous expanse with no road access. Linton Lake pooled on its outer fringe. I told Marge that, more than anything else, I wanted to spend a few days alone in that wilderness.

Oddly enough, I made my first foray into the Three Sisters Wilderness with half a dozen other people. Upon landing in Eugene, I had enrolled in alpine school in order to learn how to safely climb big mountains. Bagging Broken Top was the climax of that training. The ascent was thoroughly enjoyable, as was the company of my fellow climbers, but it didn't satisfy the nameless desire burning deep within. For that I needed to go alone into the wild.

A few weeks later, Marge dropped me off where the Pacific Crest Trail crosses McKenzie Pass Road.

We agreed that she would pick me up at the Linton Lake trailhead in five days. With minimal food and gear stuffed into an old Boy Scout rucksack, I hiked along the trail for a day and a half. On the second day I stopped for lunch, enjoying the company of a wood thrush singing from a nearby bush while I considered my next move. I knew I would have to leave the main trail soon in order to loop back around towards Linton Lake and make the pickup on time. It was just a matter of where and when. An hour later, I was bushwhacking down a steep incline leading to Linton Meadows. I lost my footing and slid a good part of the way down the slope. After brushing myself off and making sure I wasn't hurt, I finished the descent. Then I wandered through the meadows, grooving on the wild beauty all around me. That long afternoon had a dreamlike quality to it. I wandered aimlessly. It hardly mattered where I was going. Eventually I stopped and made camp along a small stream flowing into Linton Creek. And there I stayed for a couple days.

While I was sleeping that night, a bear tried to get into the food bag I had slung into the trees. Chipmunks overran my camp the next day. I didn't care. I looked up at the rocky face of Lane Plateau and saw something there akin to what I had seen on the shoulder of Mt. Baker during that hitchhiking trip five years earlier. I'd like to say that I saw God in that rocky face but that's not quite true. I saw beauty and grandeur there. I saw the power of life and death in an elemental world. I saw something for which there are no words – what some people call the sublime. The wildness around me was magnificent, yet I was afraid. I felt vulnerable. I was all by myself in a terrible, wonderful place – completely cut off from the rest of humanity. So I day-hiked to a small lake nearby just to give myself something to do, to distract myself from fear and keep from being overwhelmed by it all. That didn't work. The wild seeped into me from all directions until finally I stopped fighting it. Then I felt at home in the natural world, safely ensconced in the lap of God.

That night the meadow came alive with animals. I could barely see them – shadows dancing in the moonlight. The next day I packed up my things and headed downstream, following several deer as they drifted through the forest. They kept a hundred yards ahead of me the entire morning, only vaguely concerned about me coming along in their wake. I followed them until I was ankle-deep in a wetland. Then they disappeared. Shortly after losing the deer, the nearby Linton Creek became a torrent of whitewater as the ground fell away sharply to the left. The gentle banks of the creek transformed into a steep and treacherous ravine. I took a narrow game trail across a rockslide that dropped into the angry stream. Then I heard rocks falling behind me. I turned, looked up and saw a mountain lion. Our eyes locked for a split second before the wildcat scrambled up and out of sight. After that I finished the rest of my descent to Linton Lake. There I stayed another day before hiking out. As scheduled, Marge appeared at the trailhead at noon to pick me up. I stepped into the car glad to see her yet feeling like a different person – different from the one that had stepped out of the car five days earlier.

For lack of a better term, I would call my brief sojourn at Linton Meadows a mystical experience – the core of it, anyway, in those wonderful yet terrifying moments when I looked up to the rocky face of Lane Plateau and felt the presence of something greater than myself. In her book, *Mysticism*, Evelyn Underhill describes the mystical experience as "A joyous apprehension of the Absolute." That comes as close as anything can to explaining what I felt that day. In his book, *The Varieties of Religious Experience*, William James defines encounters like this as a "sudden realization of the immediate presence of God." Then he goes on to say: "Certain aspects of nature seem to have a peculiar power of awakening such mystical moods. Most of the striking cases which I have collected have occurred out of doors." Certain aspects of nature, indeed.

Time passes. Life is full of distractions, detours and dead ends. Marge didn't like living so far away from her family so we packed up our old Datsun in the summer of '81 and headed back east. We got married along the way, while staying with friends in Denver, Colorado. Then we drove all night to Chicago, dodging thunderstorms that prowled the Great Plains beneath a partial eclipse of the moon. And for a while we were happy. But Chicago was a tough town, and we hit it just as the economy was tanking.

After several stressful years working in her field – burn care, intensive care, and oncology – Marge stepped away from nursing. She took a part time job as a waitress in a pizza joint. I scrambled for work, finally putting on a tie to play assistant manager in a chain bookstore about half an hour by bus from our new home. We lived in a studio apartment in the near north end of Chicago where the sound of gunfire on a sultry summer night was not uncommon. I worried about Marge, who appeared to be coming apart at the seams. I wasn't quite sure what was wrong with her. Then it occurred to me that I needed to create a more stable life in order for Marge to be happy and our marriage to work. That's when I got it in my head to move back to New England and open a bookstore selling used books. Marge liked the idea. She would have preferred moving back to Ohio to be even closer to her family, but a bookstore in New England was a good second choice. So off we went in the summer of '82 to start yet another new life for ourselves.

Creating the bookstore from scratch took a lot more time and energy than I though it would, but I like books, didn't mind the work, and enjoyed interacting with readers. The better part of another year slipped by. Occasionally Marge would take care of business while I sat at a table in the back room, pounding out short stories or yet another version of my hitchhiking novel on a portable typewriter. I published a few things and that made me feel like I had potential as a fiction writer, but Marge wasn't happy. No, she wasn't happy at all. Her homesickness only grew worse, and it soon became clear that what she wanted and what I wanted out of life were two entirely different things. We fought, we made up, then fought some more until finally Marge said she was moving back to Ohio, with or without me. "Fine," I told her, "Then go." And that was the end of our marriage. I chauffeured her to her parents' place back in Ohio because I was afraid of her making the trip alone in such emotional distress. But a few days later I flew back to Burlington, Vermont by myself to resume work in the bookstore. We talked regularly on the phone for a while thereafter, but I never saw Marge again. The lawyers did the rest.

I spent the following autumn and a long winter engaged in self-destructive behavior: sex, drugs and alcohol – the usual demons. The bookstore barely survived it. Emotionally I teetered back and forth between guilt and despair, occasionally breaking into the kind of hedonistic elation that goes well with a bottle of wine. I danced with scores of college girls, occasionally taking one home. I read a lot of modern literature: Jean-Paul Sartre, Albert Camus, Heinrich Boll, John Hawkes, Henry Miller, and lots of Beat poetry, of course. That both helped and made things worse. While partying hard, I was told by an attractive young woman that I think too much. After giving the matter careful consideration, I concluded that I was not thinking enough.

The following spring, with a finalized divorce in the rear view mirror, I started cleaning up my act. I leaned heavily upon my new friend Andrew. He was a fellow seeker with a penchant for rational thought and an abiding interest in Zen Buddhism. We had a lot of engaging conversations about life, meaning, and what is real. In time I befriended another fellow, Richard, who appeared at face value to be a nihilist punk but in reality was much more. Then along came Mary, a wired-for-action woman with existentialist leanings who understood my angst. I got to know a bunch of poets, as well. Among the poets, I found Michael Jewell to be the most interesting, simply because he too was a spiritual wanderer. Thanks to the bookstore, I developed an elaborate network of friends whose interests went beyond partying and getting laid. Whether I did this consciously or unconsciously is a matter of debate. But one thing was clear: the more I got my act together, the more interest I took in spiritual matters.

About this time, I fell upon the writings of a Trappist monk, Thomas Merton. Not sure how this came to pass. I probably cracked open one of his books as it was coming across the counter at my bookstore. In a short discourse on how spiritual wanderers are tested, Merton called the desert the refuge of the devil, the country of madness, the home of despair. According to Merton, it is up to us "to wage war against despair unceasingly." It was the right advice at the just right time, so I read more of his work. The more I read the more I was inspired by it. And for a moment I actually considered becoming a monk. But to do that it would be necessary to join some kind of organized religion. No, that wasn't for me.

Alaska! The wilderness is where I had encountered the divine before. Why not completely immerse myself in it? I only needed the bare essentials to get by. Yeah, I had enough woods skills to survive in the wild. What was holding me back? All I had to do sell my bookstore and use the proceeds from it to reach that wide-open country far north, where I would build a cabin and live off the land in wild solitude. I immediately started making plans. Fortunately, I did a little research before putting my store up for sale. I read about how one fellow had done exactly what I planned to do only to die in the Alaskan bush from starvation and hypothermia. That's when I realized that I was guilty of hubris – of thinking so much of myself as a *spiritual* creature that I ignored my basic animal needs. And it seemed like the entire universe was breaking into belly laughs as I came to this realization. It was a cosmological humiliation to be sure. So I discarded the idea of running off to Alaska and focused upon operating my bookstore instead.

During the mid-80s I took short forays into the nearby Green Mountains to satisfy a growing desire to get closer to the wild. At the same time I met a smart, beautiful woman named Judy who encouraged me to do so. Judy had read Martin Buber, Thomas Merton and other religious writers so she knew from the very beginning of our relationship what I was all about. No easy task. Later on I had the considerably easier task of providing her with emotional support as she reinvented herself, transforming from a newly divorced housewife into an educated professional. All I had to do, really, was stay out of her way.

As the bond between Judy and I had grew stronger, and the bookstore plodded along, I went into the woods on a regular basis. Usually it was only for an early morning excursion to fish a mountain brook before opening the store. Every once in a while, I broke away to immerse myself in wildness for several days at a time. Pagan fishing I called it, ironically, because at the heart of all these outings was a desire to discover the divine in nature. And yes, the divine did appear during these outings, if only for fleeting moments here and there when I least expected it.

In due time I went deep, following a favorite stream back to its source. That took me to a small, wooded, hard-to-reach summit that became a sacred place to me. "When you go deep, following a winding river to its source," the Chinese poet Hsieh Ling-yun once wrote, "You're soon bewildered, wandering a place beyond knowing." And so it was. The more I wandered, the more I wondered until I could no longer distinguish between the two.

Meanwhile I started reading nature essays by Joseph Wood Krutch, Barry Lopez, Annie Dillard, Ed Abbey, and the like. I discovered in even the most secular of nature writers a reverence for the wild that complemented my spiritual wandering. I came into the writings of Henry David Thoreau, of course, whose famous book *Walden* hadn't impressed me when I had first read it years earlier. "The infinite bustle of Nature of a summer's noon, or her infinite silence of a summer's night, gives utterance to no dogma," Thoreau wrote in his journals, and I knew exactly what he meant by that. I'd been there. I had experienced it firsthand. Then, like the truly wild man that he was, Henry also said: "I do not prefer one religion or philosophy to another... I like Brahma, Hari, Buddha, the Great Spirit, as well as God." As a fellow wanderer, I couldn't have agreed more. Even the most elaborate belief system is but a gateway to the wild. Religions and philosophies are only fingers pointing at the moon – sketchy pathways leading to what is real. Wild nature is the first, the last, the only reality.

5. The Cult of Alders

Judy and I were married in our living room by a justice of the peace exactly three and a half years after we met. Both of us had been burned by previous bad marriages so we didn't rush to commitment even though it was clear a few months into the relationship that we were meant for each other. It was clear to me, anyhow. Judy was a bit more skeptical. At any rate, we married in late autumn of '88 after living together for a while. Then my life changed in ways that I never could have foreseen.

A few months after getting married, I sold the bookstore and went to work as a tour leader for Vermont Hiking Holidays. Along with a dozen other tour leaders, I took urbanites on day hikes during the warmer months. For many of our clients, it was their first time in the woods. I shared my love of the wild with them during these outings, and thoroughly enjoyed this so-called work, but something wasn't quite right with me. During my second year in the field, I grew restless for reasons I couldn't understand much less explain to anyone. That didn't make sense. I had a good marriage, a dream job, and plenty of time to write off-season. What was there not to like? But it wasn't about liking or disliking. Something else was churning deep inside me.

"What do you want?" Judy asked me point blank one day, picking up on my restlessness.

"I want to go to Alaska," I blurted out to my own great surprise. And that's how the journey began. I immediately dismissed it as a foolish and impractical idea, but Judy wouldn't drop the matter. In time she made me see that going to Alaska was exactly what I had to do.

It wasn't so much about beginning a new journey as it was finishing an old one – one that had begun when I was sixteen. My relationship with God was unresolved. What better place to address deeply spiritual matters than alone in a vast wilderness? Shortly after divorcing Marge, I had considered moving to Alaska, but that desire had a self-destructive aspect to it. Now I just wanted to go there for a short while – a brief sojourn – just long enough to sort a out few things in my head and perhaps encounter the divine as I had in Linton Meadows a decade earlier. Judy couldn't have been more supportive. So I started making plans.

Life is what happens while we're making plans. To fund a trip to Alaska, I needed a full-time year-round job not a seasonal one. Steve, my boss at VHH, promised me a full-time position in the office, but an unexpected downturn in the economy delayed that. Another year passed before I started that job and could get serious about making a trip to Alaska happen. That was probably for the best. The extra year gave me time to finish writing a non-fiction version of my hitchhiking trip out west, prepare myself better for the coming adventure, and make sure that I had my head screwed on right. "People disappear in the bush all the time," Alaskans like to say. I wanted to make sure that I didn't become one of those people.

Alaska! The word still intoxicated me. I couldn't imagine a better place to encounter the divine than that wide-open country up north. I had felt the tug of it while standing dockside in Seattle as a 20-year-old hitchhiker. The only thing that had prevented me from stepping onto an Alaska-bound boat back then was a lack of money. By the summer of '92, I had secured a round-trip airline ticket to Juneau, had reserved a bush plane to get me from Juneau to the Endicott River Wilderness, and had acquired all the provisions and equipment necessary to survive for several weeks in the wild. With Judy's blessing, I was headed for Southeast Alaska. There I would resolve my spiritual concerns once and for all. There I would confront my Maker or die trying.

I began to seriously question the wisdom of this undertaking as the pilot strapped me into the back seat of a small plane headed for the bush. I suspected that I wasn't really equal to the task despite the fact that I carried a heavy revolver, a large can of bear repellant, and 125 pounds of food, clothing and equipment. On the ground later on that day, with both feet inside the rear track of an Alaskan brown bear, I knew for a fact that I was in over my head. While hopping out of that track, I freaked out. I hoisted all my food into the trees, fifteen feet off the ground, before it occurred to me that I was going to need it. Slowly I regained my senses. Then I lowered the food bags, repacked everything, and finished my trek to the river. Yeah, the river was a much better place to make camp than on a bear trail. Be cool, I told myself. I had to keep my wits about me in order to stay alive.

In my foolishness, I had gone to Alaska to confront my Maker or die trying. It soon became apparent that I would simply die trying. Every attempt I made to venture farther upstream from the relative safety of my base camp near the mouth of the river was thwarted. That is, I got myself into precarious situations time and time again. Only a strong desire to get back home to my loving wife kept me from "disappearing." The impenetrable alders, the raging torrent I tried to cross, relentless rain, and the bears that roamed the area all proved to be greater challenges than anticipated. I spent the better part of my first week in the bush just keeping body and soul together. There was no time for delving into spiritual matters.

I was alone in Alaskan immensity, completely cut off from the rest of humanity. The sense of vulnerability that I had first experienced during my very brief sojourn in the Three Sisters Wilderness a dozen years earlier was now a way of life. "It is in solitude," the mid-20th century outdoorsman Sam Campbell once wrote, "In quiet communion with nature, that we reach most deeply into truth." And that is exactly what was happening. But the truth I had sought and the truth I was learning were two completely different things. Face-to-face with the harsh reality of wildness – a reality that I could not afford to ignore – I was befuddled. How could the natural world be so beautiful yet terrible at the same time? How could the wild be so simple yet completely indecipherable? And where was God in all this?

I had gone into the Alaskan backcountry to confront my Maker, but He was nowhere to be found. There was only wildness everywhere, and the sound of wind howling through the narrow Endicott River Valley. It was a menacing sound, making it clear to me that the forces of nature were far greater than my self-asserting ego. And when it stopped, the whole world fell into an ear-shattering silence, broken only by the occasional scream of a bald eagle or the haunting croak of an unseen raven. Silence. Profound silence. The credo-busting silence that I had first encountered in a church at midnight as a 16-year-old seeker was back in full force. But now I knew that silence was the only answer I was going to get to my cosmic "Why?" So I responded to it the only way I could: by casting a line into a side-pool of the Endicott River, roaming aimlessly through the climax forest, lounging in muskeg bogs, and tossing sticks onto a crackling fire at midnight. In other words, everything I did became a prayer to the wild.

Thomas Merton had warned me: "The solitary is a man who has made a decision strong enough to be proved by the wilderness: that is to say, by death. For the wilderness is full of uncertainty and peril and humiliation and fear…" Fair enough. I had asked for it and the wild had delivered. It gave me exactly what I wanted: the truth. I went into the Alaskan wilderness to confront my Maker or die trying, but no such confrontation had been forthcoming. Nor did I die. I was checkmated instead by wild reality, and shown to be the utter fool that I am. I, *Homo sapiens*, am the brainiest creature roaming the earth, but hardly the be-all and end-all of existence. If I died tomorrow, the world would go on. Even if all of humankind perished with me, the world would go on.

And yet, and yet... this harsh, beautiful world somehow feels right to me. It is my home. Gazing beyond the campfire to the glaciers rising sharply out of the sea, I felt a deep kinship with my prehistoric ancestors who must have questioned their place in the greater scheme of things the same way I do. I wear wools and polyester thermals instead of fur skins, and I carry a gun instead of a spear, but the landscape remains largely the same, as do the questions. Then it came to me in a flash: I love this wild world! And with that affirmation, all confusion dissipated.

Returning to civilization, to the complex machinations of my own kind, was just as hard as surrendering myself to wildness had been. No, it was harder. I had converted to the cult of impenetrable alders and eagles screaming, and from that wild reality there was no going back. But I hadn't disappeared into the Alaskan bush. That meant a quick plane ride back to Juneau, my revolver stashed in a locking gun case, and immersion in humanity again. Humanity, yes, with its myriad worldviews and conflicting unrealities. How could I explain to anyone what had happened to me in the bush? More to the point, how could I make sense of that experience? Where was the language for it? For weeks I had lived in the lap of God – most of the time without even realizing it. At the airport back in Vermont, I fell into Judy's arms and, to my own great surprise, burst into tears. Only then did it occur to me that it would take months, years, perhaps the rest of my life to articulate what I now knew deep in my gut.

"I am a part of the whole which is governed by nature," the philosopher and Roman emperor Marcus Aurelius wrote over 1,800 years ago. "By remembering, then, that I am a part of such a whole, I shall be content with everything that happens," he concluded with stoic resolve. Yes, I too recognized that I am a part of nature, as I emerged from the bush, but no feeling of contentment "with everything that happens" came as a result. On the contrary, I became deeply disturbed by the yawning chasm between the wild reality that I had been forced to accept while I was in the bush and twisted versions of it that people embrace while safely ensconced in the developed places. Yet I knew better than to declare myself a righteous believer and dismiss every other worldview outright. I knew all too well that I held no monopoly on truth. In fact, I could barely comprehend wild reality. And my understanding of it was extremely vague, more mystical than rational, which does no one else any good. Per usual, whenever words like "Truth" or "Reality" or "God" come into play, complete understanding is elusive, and all attempts to explain the world fall victim to common sense.

6. God's Nature

The harsh beauty of the Alaskan wilderness convinced me that all cynicism and bitterness is unwarranted, that my teeth-gnashing *Why?* shouted into the world was, to some extent, misdirected moral judgment. I was angry at God for making the world the way it is, for making me so self-aware yet pathetically mortal, for allowing diseases, disasters, and the countless evils practiced by humankind. I went into the bush to confront my Maker or die trying, and a part of me died there – the part that wanted to *confront*. In the great and terrible silence that answered my question, I was completely disarmed. And from the rubble that had been my carefully constructed worldview, there emerged a new, much wilder self that wanted only to see the world the way it is and revel in it.

One thing became clear to me while I was in the bush: God and nature are inextricably entwined. To embrace one is to embrace the other. To reject one is to reject the other. The logic of it, laid out by a Christian mystic long before I came along, is simple. "If God were not in everything, nature would not function," Meister Eckhart said. Nothing has ever made more sense to me. And that, I suppose, is why I went to

Alaska in the first place. But nature is as inscrutable as God is. In response to the ultimate question, the only question that really matters, there can be only silence. Every other answer is a misrepresentation of what is real. But that doesn't keep us from trying, does it?

Two thousand years ago, a man named Jesus of Nazareth walked among us, espousing a philosophy of love. Like Gautama, the father of Buddhism, Jesus did not concern himself with metaphysical matters. Unlike Gautama, Jesus had a more otherworldly solution to the problem of human suffering. He focused on the souls of men and women, and promised the kingdom of heaven to those who rejected all worldly matters and practiced brotherly love. He referred to God as the Father, leading his disciples to believe that he was the Son of God – the Messiah as promised by Judaic prophets. He ran afoul of the authorities and was crucified for the threat he posed. After that his followers called him Jesus Christ. And a whole new brand of monotheistic religion spun off from Judaism as a consequence – one known as Christianity.

Six hundred years after Jesus, the prophet Mohammed walked the earth, spreading the word of Allah – the one and only God. Like Jesus, he also ran afoul of local authorities. Like Moses and his Chosen People, Mohammed left the place where he and his ideas were not welcome. Mohammed and his people went from Mecca to Medina in an exodus called the *hejira*. And just like the New Testament of the Bible that is based upon the teachings of Jesus, *The Koran*, written by Mohammed and inspired by God, became the moral authority for all those who embraced it. Then

Islam, yet another strong branch of monotheism, arose in the Middle East.

What does all this tell us? Only that monotheism has spread like a wildfire since ancient times, and that morality is an integral part of it. The God of Abraham is alive and well, it seems, and the good/evil dualism of Zoroaster has stayed with us. But all this runs counter to what the wild teaches... or does it?

Even the most elaborate moral/religious system cannot completely divorce God from nature. All it can do is shift the focus of our attention elsewhere. Ultimately in any *rational* discourse concerning the nature of things, the relationship between God and the natural world must be addressed. And that's what happened during the Late Antiquity and Early Middle Ages, long before any angst-ridden, modern philosophers like me came along.

When we utter the word "God," what is it exactly that we are trying to say? And what is this phenomenon that we call nature? In the Roman Empire during the third century, a philosopher/mystic named Plotinus gave this matter considerable thought. Borrowing heavily from Plato, Plotinus concluded that the natural world emerges from an all-pervasive Soul, which stems from a set of pure ideas called Intelligence, which comes into being from The One. "It is by The One that all beings are beings," he wrote in the *Enneads*. As Plotinus saw things, "The One is without form, even intelligible form." This is heavy stuff even for a modern thinker like me to contemplate. It's hard to imagine anyone thinking this way in a time when so many others still embraced a pantheon of gods.

Plotinus wasn't the only thinker of late antiquity influenced by Plato. The Jewish philosopher Philo of Alexandria, who lived about the same time as Jesus, preceded him. Plotinus was followed by the Christian theologian Saint Augustine, who studied Plato and pondered ultimate things just as the western half of the Roman Empire was coming apart at the seams. We call these and the many other thinkers like them *Neo-Platonists*, but it was Plotinus who pressed Plato's metaphysics to the limit. "The One is not a being because it is precedent to all being," Plotinus wrote. The Absolute, whether it is framed as God, nature or something else, doesn't get any more abstract than that.

It is difficult, if not impossible, to contemplate the nature of things without considering their origins. That is why creation myths abound in the world's great religions, and why the Absolute always comes into play, one way or another. This fact was not lost on the ninth century Irish theologian John Scotus Erigena. He took the relationship between creation and the Absolute one step further. In his book, *The Division of Nature*, he wrote: "When we are told that God made anything, what we should take this to mean is that God is in all things." This is Neo-Platonism at its finest. Erigena challenges us to think about God as something more than a Maker of the natural world, or a Supreme Being lording over it. Like Plotinus, Erigena believed that God is everything.

Erigena's God is "both Everything and Nothing," the contemporary religious scholar Karen Armstrong says in her book, *A History of God*. "The two terms balance one another and are held in a creative tension to suggest the mystery which our word 'God' can only symbolize," she goes on to write. Erigena *reasoned* his way to God, thereby making Him the greatest of all abstractions, thus awakening in the Christian world a theological movement that was already well underway in Islam.

When Arabs came into contact with Greek science and ideas, *falsafah* emerged in their culture. Falsafah is the Arabic equivalent of the Greek word "philosophia," which entails rational discourse in the pursuit of natural law. The *faylasufs* were Islamic thinkers who wanted to fuse reason with the revelation of *The Koran*. Al-Kindi was the first among these thinkers, followed by al-Farabi, al-Ghazali, and many others. As Karen Armstrong points out, "The Faylasufs were attempting a more thoroughgoing merging of Greek philosophy and religion than any previous monotheists." Foremost among these theologians was Ibn Sina, better known as Avicenna to the West. "God is a Necessary Being," this eleventh century Persian thinker declared, going on to say: "When it is stated that He is a Necessary Being, this means that He is a Being without a cause, and that He is the Cause of other than Himself." Simple enough, but this begs the question: How can we know any of this beyond what is revealed to us through sacred texts? How can we be certain that God defined this way even exists?

The Scholastics, the rational thinkers of medieval Christendom, took the metaphysical baton from the Faylasufs and ran with it. Many of them, like Saint Thomas Aquinas, came up with elaborate proofs of God's existence after giving Him all kinds of superlative qualities: omniscience, omnipresence, and so on. Others took a more mystical approach. "Of God himself can no man think," the anonymous author of *The Cloud of Unknowing* wrote. "How am I to think of God himself, and what is he? I cannot answer you except to say 'I do not know!' For with this question you have brought me into the same darkness, the same cloud of unknowing where I want you to be!"

Yes, indeed – the cloud of unknowing. All godtalk, it seems, is purely speculative. There is no way for us to know *rationally* what God is or is not, and the revelations of sacred texts are always somewhat vague concerning God's nature, if they address it at all. But what about nature itself? Surely the more we learn about nature, the closer we come to understanding the most fundamental truths about the world we inhabit and the universe at large. Scientific facts are robust. Science shakes off idle speculation like a dog shaking off fleas. Wouldn't it be better to take a strictly scientific approach to the matter and leave all this godtalk behind? That would certainly be the case if God and nature weren't inextricably entwined.

"It is God's nature to be without a nature," Meister Eckhart wrote, which no doubt seemed heretical to most of the people living during his time. Those who want only to glorify God revel in superlatives like All-Knowing, All-Powerful, and All-Good. They shower God with attributes that make Him an ideal version of us. But this seems to me like the ultimate idolization – a verbally graven image. It is the anthropomorphic urge of our ancestors expressed in adjectives instead of stone. Yet Eckhart's paradoxical statement does not satisfy me the way those superlative adjectives do. I am as deeply disturbed by the playful quality of Eckhart's description of God. I want God to be *something*. All the same, the reasoning fellow in me agrees with my more mystical self that a God-without-a-nature makes perfect sense. If all nature is rooted in this phenomenon that we call God, then one thing must certainly be true: whatever precedes nature cannot *be* nature.

Does this make God supernatural? That is the assumption made by the vast majority of religious people, but to separate God from nature seems to me the most profound absurdity. That is like saying that a mother or a father is qualitatively different from his/her child. On the contrary, mother and father share a likeness with a child that is defined by their relationship. But God cannot be too much like human beings in particular, or even animals in general, because God must have a likeness to all things in nature. That makes God far greater than words like "mother" or "father" or "child" could ever express. That makes God far greater than any of the words that we use to express anything in nature. What other words are there? The term "supernatural" makes no sense. God is Absolute. That's all we can say.

Indeed, any inquiry into God's nature is a venture into the absurd. As the author of *The Cloud of Unknowing* said in his/her fit of honesty while thinking about what God is: "I do not know!" We want to define God because that would explain everything. That would answer the ultimate question and liberate us forever from all uncertainty. But every serious attempt to define God only leads us into the meaningless quagmire of words themselves.   Plotinus called the primary source of things "The One" which is, when you think about it, the same as saying nothing at all. Erigena considered God to be everything and nothing, which again gets us nowhere.   The word "Brahman" says just as much, as does the word "Tao."   Every definition of God, constructed as they are with words, is a tacit admission that we simply do not know.   It is better, I think, to revel in God's silence.

7. Natural Theology

For thousands of years, what we knew for a fact about the world was very limited, and reason played a minor role in our understanding of it. What we knew about God and the world He created came to us largely by way of revelation. Like me in my teenage madness longing to know how I fit into the greater scheme of things, humankind looked to the stars for clues regarding its nature and destiny. The heavenly bodies overhead were taken at face value. It appeared that the sun, moon, stars and planets all revolved around the earth. Since human beings play such a dominant role in this world, it was only natural to assume that it is all for us, that we are the center of the universe. And from that it was easy to believe in an anthropomorphic God – one created in our own likeness. After all, God must be a lot like us in the distinctly *human* drama being played out at the very center of things.

The Copernican Revolution marked the end of that drama. The world changed in 1543 when a Polish astronomer and mathematician, Nicholas Copernicus, published *On the Revolutions of the Heavenly Spheres*. In that book, Copernicus put forth a strong argument for a *heliocentric* universe. In other words, the earth revolves around the sun, not the other way around. To many living at the time, this incursion of science into religion seemed like the ultimate insult to humankind. And to some extent it was. After all, how can the human drama be all that really matters if the world we inhabit is not the center of the universe?

The Copernican Revolution is a misnomer. It can be called a revolution only if one thinks on a grand scale, seeing the gradual unfolding of human understanding over thousands of years. This revolution took place over 150 years. Copernicus died shortly after his theory was published and several decades went by before the Church even considered it a serious threat. Tycho Brahe, Galileo Galilei and others continued looking skyward, using mathematics and a newfound instrument called a telescope to speculate about the nature of the universe. Those fellows caused a stir to be sure. But the revolution wasn't complete until Isaac Newton published *Mathematical Principles of Natural Philosophy* in 1687, expounding his universal laws of gravitation. Even then, it took a while for the bulk of humankind to process the reality of all this. In fact, there are people living today who still don't get it. Big ideas take a long time to sink in.

The Italian philosopher/monk Giordano Bruno was an early convert to the Copernican worldview and an outspoken advocate of the heliocentric theory at the heart of it. "Thus is the excellence of God magnified and the greatness of his kingdom made manifest," he declared in the late 1500s, "He is glorified not in one, but in countless suns; not in a single earth, a single world, but in a thousand thousand, I say in an infinity of worlds." And for that, as well as his belief that God is manifest in the physical universe that He created, the Church burned Bruno at the stake.

Bruno's take on the intimate relationship between God and nature was not new. As Thomas Merton points out in a slender volume called *The Wisdom of the Desert,* others had been finding God in nature since the early days of Christianity. When someone asked St. Anthony, a 4th Century desert ascetic, how he could be happy when deprived of the consolation of books, he replied: "My book, O philosopher, is the nature of created things, and any time I want to read the words of God, the book is before me." Many people see the natural world this way. But a few thinkers, like St. Anthony and Bruno, press this notion to its logical conclusion.

While some people take the night sky at face value, others find there certain truths about the world in which we live. Science is the gradual accumulation of facts about the natural world – facts that are difficult to deny. Both religion and philosophy are attempts to make sense of the world and help us find our place in it. We do this in accordance with what we *believe* to be true. But belief is not truth. When the facts that a mathematician, astronomer, or any other scientist hands us conflict with a belief system, it is time to give that belief system an overhaul.

This is not to say that we should live by scientific facts alone. That is impossible. Science is a process, not a belief system. It is a process that never ends. We will never know everything there is to know about the universe. We will never reach a point where we will know enough things for a fact to postulate a strictly scientific worldview. So we still have to *believe* in something. That much said, we ignore scientific facts at our peril.

In the seventeenth century, a French mathematician, scientist and philosopher named Blaise Pascal wrestled with the apparent contradictions between scientific facts and his own deeply religious beliefs. In *Pensées* he wrote: "Nature is an infinite sphere whose center is everywhere and circumference nowhere." This sounds like the kind of thing one would expect any modern-day atheist to say, but Pascal adds: "In short it is the greatest perceptible mark of God's omnipotence that our imagination should lose itself in that thought." Indeed the contemplation of *infinity*, in either religious fervor or scientific inquiry, is enough to severely tax the imagination. It is enough to drive anyone to the edge of sanity. Our brains are simply not built for it.

The contemplation of infinity, as Pascal tried to show, is ultimately the contemplation of the Absolute. Nothing encourages this more than a gaze deep into the cosmos. Once it became clear that the night sky is full of stars, virtually countless, each like our own sun and incredibly distant from each other, it was easy for some people to dismiss the idea of God. But for others it was more difficult to do so. There is no need for God in a *finite* universe – one in which the laws of nature are inviolable, the stars can easily be counted, and nothing really changes. It is only when *infinity* comes to mind that we are forced to think the unthinkable, to consider all possibilities, thus contemplating the Absolute.

I become just as lost in infinity as Pascal was. Like most people, I am drawn to simpler notions. I want God to be like me – something to which I can relate – and I want his creation to be fixed and intelligible. Either that or allow me to dismiss the idea of God altogether. God the creator of a known world, or no God at all – the matter should be that easy. The contemplation of the Absolute in an infinite universe makes my head explode. It is beyond my ability to grasp. It is beyond reason, which is deeply disturbing to those of us who have seen the dark side of un-reason and don't ever want to go there again.

In the late 17th century, Newton clinched the Copernican worldview with his universal laws of gravitation. By then the scientific method had been firmly established in Western Europe, bringing to light undeniable facts at a frightening pace. The Age of Reason, also known as the Enlightenment, was underway, challenging a strictly religious worldview that had prevailed for centuries.

In response to the realities presented by scientists, some religious thinkers turned to natural theology – the application of reason and natural philosophy to spiritual matters. At the forefront of this trend was an English freethinker named John Toland. In his book *Christianity Not Mysterious*, he asserted that "the use of reason is not so dangerous as it is commonly represented," and many other freethinkers of the time agreed with him. Such people insisted that there is no real conflict between science and religion, between reason and revelation. "I assert that what is once revealed," Toland went on to say, "We must as well understand as any other matter in the world, revelation being only of use to inform us, whilst the evidence of its subject persuades us."

John Toland is closely associated with a religious movement in the 17th and 18th centuries known as Deism. The Deists saw God as a Supreme Being, or Divine Watchmaker, whose creation was both orderly and logical. They also believed that the essence of all biblical truths could be explained rationally. It was just a matter of understanding them. Voltaire and Jean-Jacques Rousseau were the most prominent Deists in France; Benjamin Franklin and Thomas Jefferson were among the many freethinkers in America who leaned towards this rational religion. In England Mathew Tindal wrote *Christianity as Old as the Creation*, which many considered a critical work of Deism. When it was released in 1730, this book became ground zero for the Deistic controversy. At the heart of this controversy was the fundamental problem of *revealed* religion itself. Not everything about Christianity in particular or revealed religions in general can be rationally explained. Miracles, for example, make no sense at all.

By the end of the 18th century, Deism had pretty much run its course, but it continued to influence freethinkers well into the 1800s. Among these was a young American minister named Ralph Waldo Emerson who shocked his congregation in 1832 when he said: "I regard it as the irresistible effect of the Copernican astronomy to have made the theological scheme of redemption absolutely incredible." Shortly thereafter, Emerson gave up the ministry and went his own way.

In 1836 Emerson published a slender volume of essays simply called *Nature*, in which he outlined a whole new way of thinking about God and the natural world. Taking the reason/revelation problem head on, he begins the book by saying: "The foregoing generations beheld God and nature face to face; we, through their eyes. Why should not we also enjoy an original relation to the universe?" As we delve deeper into nature, the conflict between science and religion fades away. Science, as Emerson sees it, is simply a way to better understand the natural world, and it is through nature that we find God. "In the woods we return to reason and faith," he wrote, adding on a personal note that when he is in the woods, "The currents of the Universal Being circulate through me; I am part or particle of God."

In the address that Emerson gave to the Harvard Divinity School a couple years later, he stated outright: "All things proceed out of the same spirit, and all things conspire with it." Then he admonished his listeners "to go alone; to refuse the good models, even those which are sacred in the imagination of men, and dare to love God without mediator or veil." This kind of talk got him into a heap of trouble with the local religious authorities. As Van Wyck Brooks reported in his book, *The Flowering of New England 1815-1865*, the Cambridge theologians reviled Emerson. To them "he was a pantheist and a German mystic, and his style was a kind of neo-Platonic moonshine." These accusations were somewhat true. Like other *transcendental* thinkers in America at that time, Emerson was heavily influenced by German Idealism, which had its roots in neo-platonic thought. Emerson's version of God as "Universal Being" would have resonated with Plotinus, Erigena, and other neo-platonic philosophers and theologians who lived during the Late Antiquity and Middle Ages. And yes, though I'm sure he would have denied it, Emerson was a pantheist to some extent. After all, he turned to nature itself to resolve the conflict between reason and faith. If that's not a pantheist then what is?

The term "pantheist" was first used in a rather obscure work written by Joseph Raphson called *De Spatio Reali*, published in 1697. By Raphson's definition, a pantheist is one who believes in a universal substance, both physical and intelligent in the Platonic sense, out of which all nature emerges. John Toland took this term from Raphson and coined it in a book that he published in 1705 called *Socinianism Truly Stated*. Over time the term "pantheism" simply came to mean: God is nature, and vice versa. Not exactly what Emerson was trying to say, but one can see why his critics accused him of it. Clearly Emerson's God was not the one described in the Bible – not God as portrayed by traditional Judeo-Christianity. Emerson's "Universal Being" isn't the least bit anthropomorphic. And it is inextricably entwined with the natural world.

Like Henry David Thoreau, Walt Whitman, John Burroughs and others who have a deep affinity with nature, I see the wisdom of Emerson's natural theology. I'm sure that it resonates with all those who sense that something more is at work in the natural world than the accidental mechanics of an utterly random universe. Emerson's little book, *Nature*, is as fresh and relevant today as it was when he wrote it nearly 200 years ago. Emerson discovered the divine in the natural world, and so have I. Now the challenge is to make sense of that discovery, to articulate what every

poet and mystic knows in his/her heart. Easier said
than done.

8. Belief and Unbelief

God is dead. That is the conclusion that many 19th century thinkers reached in the face of mounting facts, especially in the West where scientific knowledge was growing by leaps and bounds. In the bright light of science, the Judeo-Christian concept of God seemed ridiculously out of date. What role was there for God, a supernatural being similar to us in so many ways, in a universe operating according to simple mechanical laws? More to the point, the Judeo-Christian concept of God is way too anthropocentric. When it was all about us, when we were the center of the universe, it made sense that we would be the focal point of God's attention. But is it the least bit reasonable to make such a claim in a universe containing billions upon billions of stars, with countless worlds like our own revolving around them?

Darwin's book about evolution, *The Origin of Species*, was published in the mid-1800s. It did much to underscore our deep connection to the earth, but nothing to promote conventional religious beliefs. On the contrary, it made the biblical creation story seem as quaint as the myths associated with the gods of antiquity – those cartoonish gods worshipped by

Romans, Greeks, Babylonians, and ancient Egyptians. And there for a while it seemed like Man was dead as well – the human spirit reduced to the base urges of a highly evolved primate. No wonder then, that so many devout Christians saw the bones of dinosaurs taken from the ground as an elaborate ruse. What other choice did they have really?

Secular thinkers do not have much compassion for religious folk. Why should they? They have not forgotten that the Church burned Giordano Bruno at the stake for preaching the Copernican worldview, that countless others had been tortured by the Inquisition for embracing scientific facts. What compassion was there for them? No, to rational minds religion is the scourge of the earth. "It is the opium of the people," as Karl Marx once put it, designed to keep the masses ignorant and enslaved.

Like many secular thinkers, the German philosopher Arthur Schopenhauer acknowledged that humankind has strong metaphysical needs, "but religion appears to me to be not so much a satisfaction as an abuse of those needs." Therefore, the sooner that religion is done away with the better. According to people like Schopenhauer, a philosophy deeply rooted in scientific fact is a better way to go – a more rational way, a more humanistic way.

We have evolved. From this basic scientific fact it is easy for secular thinkers to deduce that we are no longer superstitious creatures who need magic to explain the great mysteries of life. Now we know a great deal about the world, and eventually we will know it all. Then we will become the gods that our ancestors once worshipped. That's our destiny. That's the assumption, anyhow, behind the worldview of another German philosopher, Friedrich Nietzsche, who believed that "the error of imaginary causes," lies at the root of all morality and religion. All we have to do to fulfill our destiny is stop confusing cause with consequence, give up the silly notion of free will, and accept ourselves for what we really are. According to Nietzsche, religion is a scourge that we should cast off. "We deny God; in denying God, we deny accountability," Nietzsche asserted, "Only by doing *that* do we redeem the world.'

Okay, perhaps Nietzsche's take on things is a bit extreme, but the message conveyed by all secular thinkers remains fundamentally the same: God is dead. He was killed by science. Good riddance. We don't need God. We are intelligent enough, evolved enough to create a just, humane, fundamentally good society without supernatural intervention. We would be better off without religion altogether. There is no point clinging to the superstitions of our ancestors. We can create a moral society without it.

I empathize with those who believe that God is dead. I understand their desire to be done with it, to cast off the shackles of superstition and live by reason alone. My own teenage madness seems incredibly foolish in retrospect – so far off the mark that I'm embarrassed by it. In a similar way, most of the intelligent, educated men and women living today are embarrassed by the vain and angry gods of the ancients. And so they should be. Such gods have no place in our world today. We moderns like to think that we have moved beyond all that silliness, beyond all mumbo-jumbo. We like to think that we have a better handle on reality than people living several thousand years ago. We have outgrown their myths, haven't we?

There is a problem here certainly. Science has killed off God as our ancestors knew Him, but has put nothing in its place. Reason, like science, is a process not a belief system. Despite the deluge of scientific facts that have arisen during the past few hundred years, reason alone gives us no viable way to make sense of the world. Without God, the history of the universe is only a random series of events and the laws of nature are arbitrary. Without some kind of Absolute, nothing makes sense. Why is there something instead of nothing? What caused the universe to come into being? To what end?

As the naturalist John Burroughs reflected a century ago, religion has not kept pace with science, and for good reason. God has to be much greater now. "I doubt if any mind can expand its conception of God sufficiently to meet the astounding disclosures of modern science," he wrote, "It is easier to say there is no God." Easier indeed, but that's no solution to the problem. How are we to make sense of the world? That remains the burning question.

"I don't believe in God," someone tells me, or they say: "There is no God," as if that is a matter of fact. Either way, I remain uniformed. What are they really saying? When one utters the word "God," what is it exactly that he or she is trying to tell me? There are countless ways to define the Absolute, and rejection of one definition is not necessarily the rejection of all others. A *personal* God? Is that the God that the secular thinker doesn't believe in? Neither do I, yet I still believe in God. God as Supreme Being? Is that what the secular thinker is rejecting? How about God as The One, The Way, Idea, Logos, Being itself, or Reason? How about God as natural order or the laws of physics? God has many faces. To reject God outright is to declare the universe utterly chaotic and everything in it an accident. But that itself is a statement of belief, isn't it? That too is an ontological stance, a presumption about Being that may or may not be true.

God the Creator – that is what a secular thinker rejects, pure and simple. Creation is what godtalk is all about, right? We know that the physical universe has evolved out of a cosmic soup, from the splitting of fundamental forces, from a singularity in time and space. And that singularity must have required a Creator. But even a statement like this is presumptuous. "The claim that God is the creator and conserver of the universe presupposes that God is ontologically distinct from the Universe," the religious scholar Michael Levine wrote in his book, *Pantheism: A Non-theistic Concept of Diety*. And that, as every pantheist knows, is not necessarily true.

One cannot make any claim whatsoever about ultimate Being without someone else refuting it. "Ontology is a messy business," Levine goes on to say, and that's a gross understatement. None of us – scientist, philosopher, or theologian – knows what we're talking about. It's all speculation. No one knows with absolute certainty what the universe is, what drives it, or how it came to be. In the final analysis, all we have are belief statements regarding it.

So then, when someone tells me that they don't believe in God, I ask them what they do believe. No matter how rational, scientific, or secular thinking that person might claim to be, their answer always slips into the ontological realm, into what-is and what-is-not. Either that or they quickly change the subject.

When pressed to it, a bona fide atheist will tell you that the universe is utterly chaotic with only the illusion of order. Everything is random, or so they say. But where do they get this idea? It is a belief like any other, based upon an attitude towards the world and their perception of things. They will tell you that it isn't a matter of belief but rather of scientific facts. Yet these facts do not tell us everything there is to know about existence. Once again, assumptions are made. No matter how outlandish or embarrassing the stories of the ancients might seem to us, we can't do much better. Every metaphysical stance requires at least one assumption, and that assumption could very well seem a little crazy to the next guy.

Agnostics back away from metaphysics altogether. They are too busy scratching out a living in this world to waste time thinking about such things. Either that or they simply don't want be bothered with it. They see all this talk about the Absolute as utter nonsense, and they don't really care how the universe came to be or how it will end. Secretly they think they are above the fray. They think morality is largely a matter of common sense. They believe that all godtalk, whether for or against, is idle speculation about things that have little bearing upon our well being, here and now.

More than outspoken atheists or secular thinkers of any stripe, agnostics come the closest to living in unbelief. Yet they still make assumptions about the world in which they find themselves. From the time they get out of bed in the morning until they fall asleep again, their actions reveal what they truly believe. One cannot get out of bed without believing in *something*, even if it is only the pursuit of happiness. Perhaps agnostics are simply more honest with themselves than atheists or theists are. At least they admit, on some level, that despite all the grey matter between our ears, we don't really know anything for certain about the world. So then, they say, let's just get on with our lives and get as much pleasure out of it as possible.

9. The Divine Cosmos

Seeing is believing. When I peered into a telescope and saw a galaxy with my own eyes for the very first time, I underwent a religious conversion. It was validation actually, of what the Alaskan bush had taught me over a decade earlier. Seeing Andromeda Galaxy, that great spiral of stars much like our home galaxy the Milky Way, was like gazing into the unblinking eye of God. Armed with information gathered by scientists over the previous hundred years, I saw more there than a blurry patch of light. I saw an island of stars in the darkness, separated from our own island by two and a half million light years. My kind didn't even exist when the light just entering my eyes left that source. I saw billions of stars swirling around a mysterious center. I saw immense concentrations of energy locked in a cosmic dance. I saw natural order on a grand scale, and a wildness that goes beyond words.

For a little over a year, I studied the cosmos like a man possessed, wandering far and wide through the night sky with the help of a 4.5-inch reflecting telescope, learning the names and relative locations of all the major stars and constellations, and finding nebulous phenomena adrift in the great sea of darkness.

Star clusters, stellar nurseries, the remnants of supernovas, and galaxies – I saw them all with my own eyes. To make sense of what I was seeing I read dozens of books on astronomy and astrophysics. I also garnered information from the Internet. The more I learned, the more my religious fervor grew. Yes, as strange as it might sound to secular and religious folk alike, science fueled my religion.

What I saw through my small telescope made real what I had only surmised to be true. Seeing a photo of a galaxy is one thing. Seeing the real thing in real time is something else altogether. It's the difference between the abstract and the concrete. And while religion is supposed to be abstract and otherworldly, what I have found deep in the night sky has been no less moving than the religious experiences I've had in Alaska, the Cascade Mountains, and other wild places. No surprise there. The night sky is a great wilderness stretching for billions of light years in all directions, largely unknown and unexplored.

In the first decade of the 20th century, a scientist named Henrietta Leavitt discovered a period-luminosity relationship in Cepheid variable stars. The American astronomer Harlow Shapley used this information to measure the distances between stars, thereby giving us a rough idea just how big the Milky Way is. How big is it? So big that Shapley believed it contained all the known stars and nebulas. But in 1924 another astronomer Edwin Hubble proved otherwise. After measuring variable stars in the Andromeda nebula, Hubble determined that they were hundreds of thousands of light years beyond the Milky Way. That made Andromeda an island of stars apart from our own Milky Way. That meant both the Milky Way and Andromeda are *galaxies*, as are many other nebula out there.

In the late 1920s, Hubble and his team of scientists at the Mount Wilson Observatory took this matter a step further. They combined direct observation of Cepheid variable stars with the spectrographic analysis of light. By doing so they determined not only the great distances between galaxies, but also their movements relative to each other. It turned out that, with the exception of a few galaxies very close by, all others are moving away from us. In other words *the universe is expanding*. About the same time that Hubble made this monumental discovery, the Belgian scientist and Catholic priest Georges Lemaître theorized that the entire universe has expanded from a single point in space and time. Later known as the Big Bang, the scientific community would have dismissed this outlandish idea outright had it not been for Hubble's findings. Indeed, seeing is believing.

Since Hubble's day more and more information has been gathered, gradually turning the Big Bang into a scientific fact. Cosmic microwave background radiation and the measurable light of very distant supernovas are two of the most compelling proofs. Few scientists today question the reality of an expanding universe, or the fact that all material entities – planets, stars, galaxies, etc. – have evolved from a densely packed knot of energy long ago. Yet most are still not willing to think of the origin of the known universe as any kind of creation event.

Some folks speculate that a multitude of universes exist and that ours is just one of them. Each one of these universes is a part of a greater *multiverse*, and each one could operate according to its own physical laws. As the self-proclaimed atheist Richard Dawkins puts it, "The multiverse as a whole has a plethora of alternative sets of by-laws." By this line of reasoning, the laws of nature that govern our universe exist by happenstance. What about a creature as sophisticated as *Homo sapiens*? Are we the result of pure chance, as well? Yes, we just happen to inhabit this universe because this one has all the conditions necessary for us to exist. This is called *the anthropic principle*. And as Dawkins likes to point out, "The anthropic principle, like natural selection, is an *alternative* to the design hypothesis." So no creation is necessary. No Creator need apply.

The astrophysicist Roger Penrose has a completely different take on the Big Bang. He sees cosmic expansion as part of a greater process. Penrose postulates that there is only one universe that it oscillates over great periods of time, expanding then collapsing into itself then expanding again. He sees the pre-Big Bang era as "some collapsing phase of the universe which in some way is able to *bounce* back into an expanding universe at the Big Bang." Black holes facilitate this, Penrose believes. Entropy, the second law of thermodynamics, gets in the way of his theory, but Penrose puts together a strong argument against the efficacy of that law in his book *Cycles of Time*. It's a theory, anyhow – one that's no more outlandish than the multiverse theory. When you think about it,

Penrose's alternative to creation makes a lot more sense.

What about creation? Is the possibility of that off the table simply because it smacks of divine intervention in an otherwise strictly physical process? Are we to assume that just because creation infers a Creator that it can't possibly be true? Other theories might be more palatable to rational and scientific minds, but does that make them any more real? What do the facts show us? Only that the universe as we know it, the entire physical universe, has evolved over billions of years from a primordial state of being. We can infer whatever we want from that. Scientists have taken us back as far as a split second away from the alleged beginning of the universe, when everything was packed into an infinitely dense singularity in space/time. Beyond that it's anyone's guess.

What do we know about the universe? According to scientists, we know this much: In the beginning there was an infinitely dense singularity consisting of one fundamental force. A fraction of a second later, this force split into two, then into the four distinct forces as we know them: strong and weak nuclear forces, electromagnetic force, and gravity. Cosmic inflation took place during that first second, at which time the universe grew exponentially. Over the millennia that followed, the universe grew at a relatively slower rate into the large-scale structure that exists today. A few minutes after that initial burst of growth, the primordial soup of the early universe cooled into a subatomic plasma that lasted for 380,000 years. The organization of atoms took place after that.

About 400 million years after physical matter came into being in the shape of atoms, stars began to form, coalescing into proto-galaxies. And these early galaxies gradually transformed into the ones that exist today. Life as we know it appeared on this planet billions of years later, and the rest is evolution as Charles Darwin presented it to us. This isn't the creation story one finds in the bible, but it is a creation story all the same. The only thing missing is a Creator, along with complete knowledge of what happened in that fraction of a second at the very beginning of things.

As every physicist agrees, the laws of physics rule the universe. But, as Einstein once remarked, the physicist "finds that the fundamental laws are simplified more and more as experimental research advances. He is astonished to notice how sublime order emerges from what appeared to be chaos." This statement contains the essence of the pantheistic worldview. Order from apparent chaos. Granted, the second law of thermodynamics insists that things ultimately break down, that order degenerates into chaos over time, that entropy will have its day. But that doesn't change the fact that order exists in nature today where it didn't exist before. What causes natural order? For lack of a better term, a pantheist calls it God. Whether natural order was created by an external force or is implicit in the fabric of the universe itself is a matter of debate. Either way, a pantheist senses sublime order in the universe just as Einstein did. All true pantheists are astonished by the existence of Nature with a capital "N." There is no apparent reason for it. Logically speaking, the universe should be embroiled in absolute chaos all the time.

The dance of order and chaos – that is what makes the natural world so remarkable, so mysterious. If it were one way or the other, either perfectly ordered or utterly chaotic, it would be much easier to grasp. It is this tension between the two that astounds us.

"Our conclusion must be that there is no positive scientific evidence for a designer and creator of cosmic order…" the astrophysicist Paul Davies recently wrote, "There is, however, more to nature than its mathematical laws and its complex order." In other words, constants exist in nature. Why is that? Why, for example, is an atom of hydrogen the same here on earth as it is everywhere in the universe? If everything is random, then how can any so-called law of physics exist for more than a fraction of a second? The only answer is that something holds those laws in place. What that something is, well, that's anyone's guess.

While pondering the origin of things, Neil deGrasse Tyson wondered how life came to be in our universe. Obviously it didn't exist in that incredibly hot plasma of the early universe, so when did it come along? More importantly, *how* did it come along? "How does a collection of molecules, even one primed for life to appear, ever generate life itself," deGrasse Tyson asked. Good question, and one to which we have no answer. An even better question is: *why* did this happen? The shift from inanimate to animate matter is a big one, indeed, suggesting some sort of intervening external force or unknown cause. The more we look into the natural world, the more phenomena like this we find. The evolutionary process is hard at work in the universe, no doubt, but there is much about it that can't be explained. We can write off dramatic evolutionary leaps as purely random events, but that's very hard to believe. For some of us, that's no more satisfying than calling those leaps magical events. Surely there must be a *reason* why things happen. Surely there must be a cause.

Evolution is all about time. "The universe *endures*," the French philosopher Henri Bergson wrote a century ago, "The more we study the nature of time, the more we shall comprehend that duration means invention, the creation of forms, the continual elaboration of the absolutely new." This concept places us squarely in a dynamic universe – one that is constantly unfolding, neither fixed in place nor purely happenstance. The natural world illustrates this every day. Everything is evolving. To see evolution taking place all we have to do is look around. All we have to do is pay attention to what is happening around us. The greatest mystery of the universe lies in the most commonplace events, like when a new species appears – something that definitely didn't exist before. That's not magic, that's nature!

Who knows what nature will do tomorrow, what our world will look like in a million years, or what the universe will be like in ten billion? Everything is on the move. We only fool ourselves when we say that we have a firm grasp on things. Even as scientists probe nature from all directions, it remains something of a mystery and always will. As Emerson said, "To the intelligent, nature converts itself into a vast promise, and will not be rashly explained. Her secret is untold." And that is why the word "God" should not be discarded as we probe deeper into the cosmos. To dismiss God as an antiquated perception of reality is to dismiss nature itself – Nature, that is, with a capital "N." For physics and science do not exist, there are no laws of nature, without the causal relationship between what *is* and what *was* that's built into the natural world.

10. God and Wildness

Nature is the dance of order and chaos, the tension between what is and what can be, the intrusion of the possible upon the probable. That is why we call it *the wild*. There is something terrifying about this, certainly. Wildness implies unpredictability, and that undercuts our sense of security. We *civilize* the world in order to make it more user friendly, more predictable – to keep wildness at bay. And yet the civilizing process itself has a wild aspect to it. After all, there is no progress without innovation, which is just another word for wild thinking, and progress is what civilization is all about. So we find ourselves in an uncomfortable situation where the very thing we fear the most is essential to our well being. It's a paradox to say the least.

In a completely ordered world, wildness would not exist. In a world where nature was held together in perfect balance, everything would happen for a reason. Then reason would be absolute. That is the world the ancients invented to fill in the gaps of understanding, to keep the unknown at bay. That is world that most of us desire – religious and secular thinkers alike. But that is not the world in which we find ourselves. Our world is fraught with indeterminacy. Our world is full of unpredictable and unforeseeable events. Even as our scientists push out the frontier of knowledge and our control of nature increases, the wild persists. Like the great unknown that constitutes the better part of the universe, the wild goes on forever. It also thrives deep within us. We only fool ourselves when we say that we have overcome it.

Freedom? Is that what we're talking about here – freedom versus determinacy? Yes and no. Freedom, like slavery, is a social construct that arises from our civilizing efforts. The wild is freedom prior to those efforts – the freedom of things in their natural state, which is also the freedom of things to behave contrary to what's expected of them. But that's impossible, isn't it? A fox will always behave like a fox, won't it? More to the point, an atom of hydrogen will always be an atom of hydrogen, right? Ah, perhaps that is a bad example, for we know that hydrogen becomes helium during the fusion process deep inside stars. What's a better example? Is the world more predictable at the subatomic level? No, quantum uncertainty confounds that. So what can we reasonably expect of a world constructed with building blocks that are themselves subject to change? Probabilities are what we have, not certainties. The wild is precisely that which confounds certainty. The wild is subatomic and cosmic possibility. It is universal.

After my brief sojourn in the Alaskan bush, I knew viscerally that God and the wild are one in the same, but rationally speaking that didn't make any sense to me. How could natural order arise from wildness?

How could they even coexist? With this paradox in mind, I wandered for years about my home range, the Green Mountains, looking for clues. "One must always cross-question nature if he would get at the truth," John Burroughs said, so that's what I did. I approached the wild from many different angles, trying to get a better handle on it. I tramped its muddy trails, cut tracks through snowy woods with my snowshoes, and fished its pristine mountain streams. I camped and hiked with family and friends, and bushwhacked alone into patches of untrammeled forest. I reveled in the wild, catching glimpses of the divine along the way. But that didn't help me make sense of it. Not really. The poet in me was fine with that, but not the philosopher. I wanted to resolve the paradox. I wanted to better understand God and the natural world. So I went deeper.

Vermont's Green Mountains are a long, relatively narrow strip of wild country running south to north. You can go up and down them but there's not much room to maneuver. While wandering the Green Mountains, one is never far away from a road or some kind of development, that is. So I ventured across Lake Champlain and into New York's Adirondacks. While studying maps of the Adirondacks, one particular patch of wild country caught my eye: the West Canada Lakes Wilderness. It is one of the largest roadless areas east of the Mississippi, giving a woods wanderer like me plenty of room to maneuver. So there I went for a week in the summer of 2002, hoping to gain a better understanding of the relationship between God, nature and humankind.

The wild always surprises. Time alone in wild places does things to one's psyche that are difficult to replicate elsewhere. I had started out very goal-oriented, on my way to West Lake, but the second day into my pilgrimage I changed my mind. I went to Lost Pond instead. A blister on the bottom of my foot the size of a silver dollar had something to do with my decision – that and the fact that my sick and aging canine companion, Jesse, was having a hard time of it. I figured we could go to Lost Pond then loop back to the trailhead from there, thus cutting our trip short. Those were my *reasons*, anyhow. But on another level I felt something else: a burning desire to leave the beaten path cutting through the wilderness. After all, I find it much easier to groove with the wild once removed temporarily from any vestige of humanity.

After a few days bushwhacking through deep woods, it suddenly occurred to me that I was approaching the paradox of wildness and natural order the wrong way. I had assumed that it was all about me, about *my* understanding of the natural world, and *my* ability to convey nature's message to others. Like Thoreau, I had perceived myself as a prophet of wildness. But awakening one morning to shafts of sunlight breaking through the canopy of the trackless forest, I suddenly realized otherwise. I wander, I wonder, I write – that is all. I have no special powers when it comes to understanding the nature of the world. I have no idea what God's plan is, or even if there is a plan. The wild is its own excuse for being. It has its own agenda. That much is clear to any woods wanderer. All the rest is merely verbiage, half-baked concepts, and the wildest speculation. But we still have to try, don't we? We have a moral obligation to ourselves to at least try to make sense of the world and find our place in it. We are too self-aware to leave the matter unaddressed.

"How natural is 'natural,'" the renowned essayist Loren Eiseley once asked, "And is there anything we can call a natural world at all?" A question like this runs counter to common sense. Nonetheless, it makes a good point. We utter the word "nature," assuming that no definition is necessary – that what we are talking about is apparent to all. But to declare what something is also suggests what it is not. What is the opposite of natural – artificial, manmade, unnatural, or supernatural? Is there anything in this world that stands apart from nature? If not then isn't the term "natural world" rather redundant? The more we think about nature, especially Nature with a capital "N," the less sense it makes. We talk about nature as if it is a self-evident phenomenon, but nothing is more subject to interpretation or open for debate.

Nature toys with us, making mincemeat of our logical constructs. This is especially true when it comes to our understanding of nature itself. As the Jewish theologian Abraham Heschel said, "Nature, the sum of its laws, may be sufficient to explain in its own terms how facts behave within nature; it does not explain why they behave at all." In other words, nature itself, Nature with a capital "N" that is, defies all analysis. The laws of nature resist any rational explanation. All we can say with any certainty is that they exist. We don't know how or why.

Talking about the particulars found in nature is one thing; talking about the whole of it is another. As the British physicist James Jeans put it so well three-quarters of a century ago: "Our studies can never put us into contact with reality, and its true meaning and nature must be for ever hidden from us." There are those among us who believe otherwise, but the facts speak for themselves. The most important fact is this: we do not know everything. And it's a pretty safe bet to say that we never will. Nature is, after all, greater than any human concept of it.

How wild is nature? Wilder than we can imagine. Evolution shows us, time and time again, that anything is possible. "Becoming is infinitely varied," the French philosopher Henri Bergson wrote in *Creative Evolution*. A close look at the diversity of life proves his point. Both the geological record and current plethora of species clearly illustrate that what is possible often comes into being regardless of all improbability. This leads some people to believe that biodiversity is as random as a throw of the dice. Yet others suspect that there is a driving force behind it all, that the self-asserting nature of life itself is no mere accident. Either way, it's clear that we live in a wild world – as wild as any world can possibly be.

According to Bergson, nature "everywhere presents disorder alongside of order, retrogression alongside of progress." The facts bare this out. One doesn't have to look any farther than a forest floor to find growth and decay, evolutionary success and failure, order and chaos. It's all there for us to see on any given day, at any given moment. And if we look deep within ourselves, we can see it as well. Collectively speaking, how have we progressed? We've come a long way since the Ice Age, yet our war zones, refugee camps, impoverished rural landscapes, and decaying inner cities are a far cry from paradise. From an evolutionary perspective, there is much room for improvement in the human matrix that we call civilization.

The wild is divine, certainly, having all the qualities associated with the concept of the Absolute. But divine wildness is not God in any conventional sense. It is not an anthropomorphic god sitting on a throne in the clouds judging people, nor is it a vague, philosophical abstraction far removed from the natural world. On the contrary, divine wildness is here and now, in our face each and every day, as immediate and concrete as nature itself. Divine wildness is all there is because it is all-inclusive, because everything in the universe is essentially wild – the stars and galaxies, the mountains and rivers, the weather, and all living things including us. Domestication, like civilization itself, is a temporary condition – a process that is never complete. In all things, even a garden lily, a dog or a cow, there exists feral possibility. Wildness is the condition of the world before *Homo sapiens* came along. And someday, when our kind is gone, all things will revert to wildness. That is nature's way, and the divine force behind it wears the word "God" quite well.

The only irrefutable facts are natural facts – what science provides on a regular basis. The only fixed laws are the laws of nature. Human laws, and the perceptions from which they emerge, are subject to change. Natural laws are immutable by definition. As the Christian theologian Charles Hartshorne wrote: "Any god with whom facts could conflict is an idol."

That leaves only one god standing: God manifest in wild nature. Everything else is human contrivance – what we *want* the world to be, not what it is. To refute this is to refute reality itself.

Curiously enough, those who embrace nature often call themselves atheists, denying that God or anything like it could possibly exist. This is understandable. The word "God" comes with a lot of baggage. It is fraught with confused and conflicting meaning. Most people, religious and secular alike, imagine a supernatural entity when the word "God" is uttered. To them God is an otherworldly phenomenon, and nature is something apart from it. People generally speak of "acts of God" as if they were isolated events upsetting the natural order of things. But, as Hartshorne so insightfully observed, "The only 'acts of God' we can identify (in spite of the lawyers) are the laws of nature." Everything else is a misrepresentation of things based upon the presumption of magic.

The world we live in is not magical, but it is mysterious. It is mysterious because we can never have all the information necessary to fully understand it. Despite the ongoing discovery of natural facts by science, unknown aspects of the universe persist. In those aspects lies true mystery – a phenomenon that we call *the wild*. And manifest in the phenomenon of wildness is a divine force we can't begin to grasp. Hence the word "God."

We cannot know all there is to know about the natural world because it is an unfinished story. It is becoming, unfolding, evolving right before our eyes. Even what we perceive as the immutable laws of nature might not be laws at all. It's hard to say. We have no crystal balls. We don't have all the information necessary to determine whether nature as we know it is temporary or permanent. We cannot fully grasp the nature of nature – nature, that is, on the grand scale that is the universe. We cannot know the fate of the universe any more than we can know the mind of God. In wildness there is indeterminacy, and we live in an utterly wild cosmos.

11. The Pantheistic Worldview

Pantheism is the belief that God and nature are inextricably entwined. Unfortunately, any simple definition of it ends there. Some pantheists wouldn't even use the word "God" to denote the fundamental force that organizes the universe because that implies a Creator – a concept they emphatically reject. Some pantheists wouldn't use the word "entwined" because that suggests that God and nature are separate entities, which undercuts their holistic way of seeing things. Indeed, the only thing all pantheists would agree on is that the divine is found *in* nature, not beyond it.

The pantheistic worldview is not easy to understand. In some ways it is a new belief system, loaded with many of the subtle and complex notions typical of our time. Part of the problem is that there is no founding father of pantheism, no prophet or guru, no sacred texts to which a self-proclaimed pantheist can turn. It is, in a sense, a worldview derivative of other worldviews. It is worldview that has slipped in and out of other more established worldviews, both religious and philosophical, for thousands of years. It is a belief system so vague, so incredibly abstract that one wonders if it is a belief system at all.

In contrast to the vagueness that is implicit in pantheism, two so-called pantheistic organizations have popped up in recent years. Harold Wood founded the Universal Pantheist Society in 1975. A couple decades later another organization known as The World Pantheist Movement spun away from it. Paul Harrison leads that one. Both organizations are environmental in their focus, making one question the *theism* of their particular versions of pantheism. A quick perusal of their websites leads me to believe that they are simply trying to create a religious/philosophical foundation for a new morality – one with rites and rituals similar to what nature-worshipping pagans practice. The attempt of both organizations to create easily digestible credos seems contrary to what pantheism is all about. Then again, that's a fairly common turn of events in the history of worldviews. They often morph into something completely different from what they started out to be.

When John Toland published a book in 1705 called *Socinianism Truly Stated*, he brought to light the term "pantheist" that had been coined by Joseph Raphson a few years earlier. But the basic concept of pantheism goes way back. Giordano Bruno's heretical vision of God being glorified by an infinite universe was quite pantheistic, as was John Scotus Erigena's claim that God is in all things. When Plotinus said that "The One" precedes all being, he obviously envisioned an immanent God – one inseparable from what is called nature. Looking farther back in history, at different places on the globe, we find the "All-pervading Power" of Taoism and the "Brahman, one and infinite" of

Hinduism. Clearly the idea of one-ness, which is the core belief in all versions of pantheism, is not new. On the contrary, it could very well be as old as humanity itself.

"Modern Pantheism as a religion begins with Spinoza," J. Allanson Picton wrote a century ago in his obscure little book, *Pantheism: Its Story and Significance*. Many pantheists would agree. When he published his landmark philosophical work *The Ethics* in 1677, Benedict de Spinoza outlined a rational worldview that placed God squarely *in* nature. Spinoza's worldview is *monistic*. That is, his God/universe is one substance in contrast to a *monotheistic* worldview where God stands apart from the world he creates. "By God, I mean a being absolutely infinite – that is, a substance consisting in infinite attributes," Spinoza wrote. Then he added: "Whatever is, is in God, and without God nothing can be, or be conceived." This is pantheism to be sure. As a consequence, Picton and many other believers have declared Spinoza the father of pantheism.

The fusion of God and nature, implied by the word "unity," is the core belief of the pantheistic worldview. In his book, *Pantheism: a Non-theistic Concept of Divinity*, Michael Levine directly addresses this matter: "The pantheist claims both that there really is order, and that there is something responsible for the order such as a Unifying principle." No pantheist would disagree with that. But the Spinozan concept of a monistic God is not essential to pantheism. "For the pantheist," Levine also wrote, "God and the world generally are not and should not be taken as intentionally equivalent." This is the difference between essence and existence, about which philosophers and theologians have been arguing for centuries. "Something about the world – namely the fact that it is taken to be an all-inclusive divine Unity – is the reason for calling the world 'God,'" Levine adds. In other words, there is a fundamental force, something divine in the natural world, from which all things arise. We call it God as a convenience. We use the word "God" for lack of a better term.

Picton may have overstated the matter when he said: "In the view of Pantheism the only real unity is God." Not everyone who claims to be a pantheist would agree with this. Not every pantheist is comfortable with the word "God," in this context or any other. After all, it carries the baggage of anthropomorphism – the *humanized* Supreme Being of Judeo-Christianity and other established religions. In fact, there are those who see pantheism as the direct opposite of any kind of *theistic* belief whatsoever. That is what leads secular thinkers like Richard Dawkins to say rather tongue-in cheek: "Pantheism is sexed-up atheism."

Is this true? Are pantheists really atheists at heart? Richard Dawkins thinks so. In his popular book, *The God Delusion*, he reasoned: "Pantheists don't believe in a supernatural God at all, but use the word God as a non-supernatural synonym for Nature, or for the Universe, or for the lawfulness that governs its workings." Ah, close but no cigar for the man who claims that all talk about God is bunk. It's true: pantheists do not believe in a *supernatural* God, but they do believe in a natural one. The divine is manifest in nature. According to a pantheist, it lies at the root of all things. Known as God, Unity, the One, or by any other name, it is still divine and it is still *in* nature. As Picton pointed out, pantheism is "the precise opposite of Atheism." While the atheist sees nature as a strictly mechanistic process devoid of any divinity, the pantheist sees all nature as divine. That's a big difference indeed.

Pantheism is as much a religion as it is a philosophy. That is evident in the pantheist's insistence that there is something divine in nature, something that orders the natural world. Not only does that natural order contradict the idea of an utterly random universe, it is also inexplicable. The divine Unity implicit in nature is far greater than any idea of God that we can conceive. This Unity is all encompassing therefore any human-like qualities projected upon it are absurd. In the pantheist worldview, there is no room for a God created in man's image. On the contrary, God must be everything.

Towards the end of his book on pantheism, Levine says that organized religions are divisive and exclusive, and churches are essentially anthropocentric. That is why he believes that "there never has been a pantheistic church and probably never will be." The all-encompassing, profoundly abstract nature of the pantheistic version of God does not give the average churchgoer much to grab hold of, nor does it seem particularly relevant to the moral challenge of daily living. Its open-endedness is something of a disadvantage in this regard, and any attempt to organize pantheism into an established credo seems to fall short of the mark. It is simply not that kind of religion. Yet it is a religion all the same.

To believe in the divinity of nature is to believe in some kind of God, however abstract that God may be. To identify Oneness or Unity as that which is responsible for what is commonly called natural order is to embrace pantheism. Beyond that it is difficult to say anything about the pantheistic worldview that can't be refuted by at least one of its proponents.

Those who believe in a Supernatural Being are not pantheists. That much is certain. Those who dismiss the divine altogether are clearly atheists. Others, who don't care to give the matter much thought, are best described as agnostics. These labels account for the vast majority of people living on our planet at any given time. As for back-to-earth nature lovers, most are really more neo-pagan in their outlook, preferring the rites and rituals of ancient animistic or polytheistic religions to the kind of abstractions that pantheism evokes. Only those who see the divine *in* nature subscribe to the pantheistic worldview. It's a quirky religion to be sure, but does that make it any less legitimate as a belief system? Is there a better way to understand the grand scheme of things?

12. The Grand Scheme of Things

Natural order seems self-evident. Most of us look at the beauty of the world – its complexity, symmetry and apparent balance – and know intuitively that nature exists apart from our idea of it. But this is not a foregone conclusion. There are those who truly believe that the patterns we find in the world do not really exist. They think everything is the result of chance. Theirs is an utterly random universe, one in which the right set of circumstances for a highly cognizant, self-aware creature like *Homo sapiens* just happens to exist. Given a different throw of the dice in that fraction of a second at the very beginning of the Big Bang, they say, the universe would be organized according to an entirely different set of physical laws and we wouldn't be here. Perhaps the universe would not be organized at all. There is no reason why it should be. Like all beliefs, there is no way to prove this. But that doesn't keep some people from believing it. So they live their lives in the illusion of order, knowing deep down inside that it is not really there. And you will not convince them otherwise.

For those of us who do not believe in an utterly random universe, natural order is real. The stars prove it, as do subatomic particles, as does the evolution of all things both animate and inanimate. But again, these so-called proofs are more a matter of revelation than reason. We know it intuitively, yes, but there is no way to say with absolute certainty that Nature with a capital "N" exists for a fact. No self-respecting scientist would ever make such a claim. It remains a faith statement, a fundamentally *religious* belief.

For those of us who believe in natural order, there are two basic ways of seeing the grand scheme of things: the principle or force that organizes the universe is either nature itself, or it comes from beyond. In theological terms, this comes down to an age-old choice: God is either immanent or transcendent. In philosophical terms, the world is either being or becoming. Sliced and diced a hundred different ways, the choice before us is Plato versus Aristotle, monism versus monotheism, eastern religion versus western. This is a gross simplification, certainly, of the great argument that we have been having with each other since the beginning of our self-awareness, but it brings to light the essential weakness of any given worldview. There are no facts, scientific or otherwise, that can help us here. When it comes to the grand scheme of things, a choice must be made – a belief of some sort must be embraced. Either/or.

Like so many thinkers before him, Ralph Waldo Emerson pondered the riddle of the one and the many, which lies at the heart of all religious/philosophical inquiry. "We see the world piece by piece, as the sun, the moon, the animal, the tree," he wrote in an essay, "But the whole, of which these are the shining parts, is the soul." The soul he refers to here is the Over-soul, which is his word for God – one that has certain pantheistic qualities. The whole about which Emerson spoke transcends all categories, descriptions and words. It is "the Eternal One" found in all things, including us.

Oneness or Unity seems to be the overriding message that all religious worldviews read into nature. The particulars give way to the whole. "His infinite simplicity admits no division and no distinction," the Christian monk Thomas Merton wrote. "God's glory fills the whole earth, and there is no place empty of him," the Jewish mystic Rabbi Nahman once said. "The Necessary Being cannot be two" the Islamic theologian Ibn Sina reasoned, "He is United and One; and no other shares with Him in that Unity." Similar sentiments pervade in the East. "God is in truth the whole universe: what was, what is, and what beyond shall ever be," we find in *The Upanishads*. "Great knowledge sees all in one," the Taoist thinker Chuang Tzu asserted, "Small knowledge breaks down into the many." From all this we can safely say that the idea of Oneness or Unity is common in religious thought. But there the agreement ends. We are still left with the problem of transcendence versus immanence, with the specific relationship between the one and the many. Is God *in* nature or does God somehow stand apart from everything that exists?

Pantheism is a belief in an all-pervading Unity – an organizing force in the universe that manifests itself in what we call the natural world. But it doesn't go much beyond that to explain the grand scheme of things. The German philosopher Arthur Schopenhauer wasn't too far off the mark when he said, "the chief objection I have to Pantheism is that it says nothing. To call the world 'God' is not to explain it." In other words, to assert the Oneness of God/nature does not directly address the classic dichotomy between transcendence and immanence. In my mind I can hear that cold-blooded atheist Schopenhauer saying: What precisely *is* this thing you pantheists call "God" anyhow? To that a dozen pantheists could provide a dozen different answers. Words fail us here. I imagine Chuang Tzu giving Schopenhauer the only good response: "The Great Way is not named." And there the matter would end.

In his book, *Pantheism: a Non-theistic Concept of Diety*, Michael Levine does his best to differentiate between the personal God of theism and the much more vague notion of God professed by pantheists. It seems to me that he only partially succeeds at this. "Theism claims God is transcendent, pantheism claims God is radically immanent," Levine writes, and that much makes sense. Then, as if to cover all the variations of the pantheistic worldview, he adds: "But pantheists need not claim that there are no transcendent aspects to the divine Unity." With this we are left scratching our heads over the pantheistic version of God much as Schopenhauer did. What exactly do pantheists believe, anyhow?

Levine tells us that a pantheistic God can be both immanent and transcendent, both in nature and beyond it. This sounds to me like *panentheism,* which is essentially a belief that all nature is part of God yet a fundamental aspect of God somehow transcends it. One could say that panentheism is just another variety of pantheism. After all, it starts from the premise that God exists in nature and builds from there. Or one could argue that panentheism is diametrically opposed to pantheism, that to place anything beyond nature is to revert back to that old, anthropomorphic God that lords over creation. In that case, panentheism is to pantheism what monotheism is to monism.

As with all inquiries into the grand scheme of things, it boils down to a matter of belief. Rationally speaking, we are out of our depth here. There is not now nor is it likely that there ever will be enough information to resolve this matter definitively one way or another. We cannot know for a scientific fact whether the laws of nature are implicit in this universe of ours or the handiwork of an external force, a Creator. We cannot know with absolute certainty whether God is immanent or transcendent. To put it bluntly: no one knows God's nature. In this regard, a pantheist is as clueless as any other theist.

I am inclined to believe that, when it comes to godtalk or any kind of ontological discourse whatsoever, we are all a bunch of blathering fools. The deep silence that arises whenever I shout *Why?* into the cosmos is commonplace, and my admission that I can't make anything out of that silence is just me being honest with myself. If I lean towards pantheism, it is only because I sense God's presence in the natural world. To be more specific, I sense in even the wildest aspects of nature an organizing force that goes beyond all scientific facts, beyond all rational explanations. While immersed in the wild, I sense something divine. My elaborate, philosophical attempts to better understand the grand scheme of things all come down to this: there is more to Nature than meets the eye. Yes, that's Nature with a capital "N" even though I have no idea what that really means. When I utter the word "God" I am admitting only that something greater than myself exists, that it is beyond my comprehension, and that it lies at the root of all natural phenomena. Other than that I haven't a clue.

"Nature is very complex indeed, and we are forever tempted to underestimate this complexity," the theologian Charles Hartshorne wrote in response to the materialistic worldview. Therein lies the crux of all religious sentiment. The materialist reduces everything to its smallest parts, dismissing the whole about which every religious person marvels. For the materialist the natural world is only so many subatomic particles bouncing around in spacetime, and the most fundamental laws of nature are mere happenstance. But that sounds pretty farfetched to me – about as real as a white-robed God sitting on a throne in the clouds, making his minions choose between good and evil. I am convinced that Nature is as real as I am, even though I don't completely understand it. The organizing force that I call God is embedded in nature. It is also within me because I too am a part of the natural world. Aside from that I am left wondering. And anything I say beyond the obvious is pure speculation.

13. A Reluctant Pantheism

Whenever my philosophical speculations become too abstract, I grab a backpack and head for a wild place. The deeper into the woods I go, the better the result, so I occasionally forsake the Green Mountains close to home and venture into the sprawling Adirondack Mountains on the far side of Lake Champlain. In 2006, while hiking the Northville/Placid Trail that crosses the Adirondacks, I went through the West Canada Lakes Wilderness. West Lake is in the middle of that wilderness, and there I had yet another encounter with the divine.

I awoke in the middle of the night to a bright moon reflecting off the still water of West Lake, and to a silence so deep that I could hear my own heart beating loud and clear. Sitting up, I listened intently to that great wild silence until I heard nothing, nothing at all. This time I posed no teeth-gnashing question *Why?* to the universe. Oddly enough, it hung there in the night air all the same – an ever-present query that was surprisingly easy for me to ignore. And without that question getting in the way, the answer became self-evident. The owls and loons broke the deafening silence with their midnight calls, snapping me back to the here and now. But in that moment when I lost myself in the moon and the immense universe stretching beyond it, I understood the world in a way that no strictly rational mind ever could.

"The eye with which you look at reality must constantly be changed," the Danish philosopher Soren Kierkegaard once said. That makes more sense to me in deep woods than any abstract theory that some philosopher, theologian or scientist could ever conjure up. Fixed viewpoints do no good. I am as guilty of systematic thought as anyone who has delved into metaphysics, chasing my own theories like a dog chasing its tail. But in deep woods, I stop thinking long enough to simply see the natural world all around me. Then things begin to make sense.

A few years after that mystical moment at West Lake, I returned to the West Canada Lakes Wilderness, tramping to lesser bodies of water close to West Lake but farther off the beaten path. There I listened once again to the great wild silence, catching glimpses of the divine as I had before. The voice of God, I'm convinced, is precisely that silence. And when we listen to it closely enough, we can hear the ultimate answer to the ultimate question. Unfortunately, that answer doesn't fit into words, so a seeker like me is left slack-jawed in the presence of the divine, no wiser in any practical sense. Practical wisdom, after all, lies in the truth that one can articulate, and no mystic can do that adequately.

In deep woods, whenever I venture alone in search of the divine, I am rarely disappointed. Only when I lift my camera and try to take a picture of it, or scrawl words on paper in an attempt to capture it, does the divine in nature escape me. As the science writer Chet Raymo says, quoting Heraclitus: "Nature loves to hide." Trying to embrace it is like trying to embrace campfire smoke. It is better to sit back and let that smoke curl effortlessly towards the sky. As a proponent of "religious naturalism," Raymo asserts that "Our response to the natural world is one of reverence and humility in the face of a mystery that transcends empirical knowing – now, certainly, and perhaps forever." I find this statement to be right on target. No doubt Raymo would make a good campfire companion.

When it comes to the grand scheme of things, honesty and humility are absolutely essential. Together these qualities keep us from making statements about matters that we don't fully understand. Honesty and humility go hand in hand. Together they check the natural inclination towards fixed credos. Without them we become lost in our own abstractions, entangled in webs of reason/unreason where everything supposedly makes perfect sense. Danger arises the moment we believe we have all the answers. Honesty and humility keep that danger at bay.

"I don't know whether this world has a meaning that transcends it," the French existentialist Albert Camus wrote, "But I know that I do not know that meaning and that it is impossible for me just now to know it." I love Camus for saying that. It's intellectually honest – a rare thing, indeed, for a reader to encounter when cracking open a book. This statement resonates with me as it resonates with anyone who looks deeply into the nature of nature. Camus often wrote of the absurd man who wants to know the unknowable. Like Camus, I too am that absurd man.

But wanting to know and actually knowing are two entirely different things, aren't they?

Curiously enough, it was the very abstract-thinking philosopher Paul Weiss who said: "If we are to arrive at what exists, we must do more than speak or think." This is something one would expect a guru found high in the Himalayas to say, not a philosophy professor teaching at some prestigious university. I am surprised by the honesty and humility of it – a punch that I didn't see coming. Is it possible that all deep thinkers feel this way? Do we all know, on some level, that the words we use to carefully construct our worldviews are only smoke? Speaking for myself, the answer is definitely yes.

Pantheism, I believe, comes as close as any worldview can to describing the relationship between God and the natural world – inasmuch as we can know such things. I should just call myself a pantheist and leave it at that. But if pressed to it, I would have to admit to being a *panentheist* simply because I'm convinced that the universe has evolved from a singularity in spacetime, leading me to believe that all nature was *created*. A creation event clearly puts some aspect of God beyond nature. That makes God a phenomenon that transcends nature while still being a part of it. It's a paradox to be sure.

I use the word "God" very loosely, of course. I am unwilling to describe God's attributes in detail because any definition of the Absolute is bound to fall short of the mark. Yet I remain deeply religious. That means I firmly believe that natural order exists, that some organizing force is hard at work in the universe.

The idea of an utterly random universe makes no sense to me. Nor does the animism of our distant ancestors, the gods of antiquity, or any anthropomorphic concept of God. Nor does the most abstract notion of ultimate Being dreamt up by some modern sage or philosopher. Hence I come to pantheism more by default than design.

I profess a reluctant pantheism – one restrained by an abiding belief that, as a *thinking* member of the human race, I must confess knowing nothing for certain. More to the point, no credo ever invented has a corner on truth. Pantheism is no exception to this, nor is *panentheism*. Every worldview, religious or secular, has built into it the inherent flaws of the human mind: the pitfalls of pure reason, the illusory nature of the senses, and our wildly fluctuating emotions. Brief moments of divine encounter notwithstanding, there are no exceptions to the rule of unknowing.

Pantheism is a natural religion. Though easily confused with nature worship or paganism, it is more a belief that the divine exists *in nature*, and that the best way to understand the natural world is through some combination of direct encounter and science. "The mass of mankind are not yet prepared for a religion based upon natural knowledge alone," John Burroughs once wrote, and that's as true today as it was a century ago. A great schism still yawns between religion and science, as if the reality of the world in which we live could only be understood one way or the other. Strictly religious and strictly secular thinkers conspire together against truth, presenting us with a choice that simply does not make sense: either God exists and this world is an illusion, or God doesn't exist and we are nothing more than the sum of our parts. That's a choice that neither I nor any other pantheist is willing to make.

"Man's quest for certainty is, in the last analysis, a quest for meaning," Loren Eiseley wrote. This is self-evident, I think. "But the meaning lies buried within himself," Eiseley goes on to say, "Rather than in the void he has vainly searched for portents since antiquity." Clearly I am as guilty of this as the next guy, having gone astray in my early teens and having wandered into half a dozen spiritual cul-de-sacs since then. Humility isn't a virtue I've cultivated, but rather a condition that has been thrust upon me by circumstances that have revealed my own foolishness. Like most people, I've done a lot of stupid things and have made a lot of bad decisions. A lifelong quest for meaning has brought me only to this: God and nature are inextricably entwined. Beyond that I haven't a clue. Hence my reluctant pantheism.

"Pantheism has its roots in mysticism," W. T. Stace wrote in *Mysticism and Philosophy.* If that's true, then surely I am as guilty as Ralph Waldo Emerson was of espousing neo-platonic moonshine. But when asked if I am a mystic, I groan at the implication of it. One is allowed to be a rational thinker or a mystic, but not both. Is pantheism a way around that? There is a long tradition of *thinking* mystics to prove Stace's point: Chuang Tzu, Plotinus, and John Scotus Erigena to name a few. Strains of pantheistic mysticism can be found in nearly every religious tradition. The same goes for the philosophy of people like Emerson and Thoreau, or the science of those like Einstein. Their worldviews also have the taint of mysticism to them. So as much as I groan at the implication of the word "mystic," I can't deny it. Even my reluctant pantheism is rife with it. Direct encounter with wild nature is, after all, the primary source of my understanding of the world. If that's not mysticism, then what is?

Having traveled a full circle in my quest of meaning and/or understanding, I return to an old favorite: Martin Buber. In one of his lesser known works, he wrote: "This is the glorious paradox of our existence that all comprehensibility of the world is only a footstool of its incomprehensibility." And that says it all. The more we delve into the matter, the more we are baffled. This is true for me, certainly. I have gone deep into spiritual matters, deep into metaphysics, and deep into the natural world only to find myself up against the great wild silence time and time again. The more I learn, the less I know for certain. The more that I think I know, the more it becomes clear that I operate according to a belief system that reaches well beyond any definitive facts. Sometimes I fool myself into thinking I have a good bead on things, but a few days alone in deep woods convinces me otherwise. In the final analysis, the answer to the ultimate question *Why?* that I once shouted into the universe lies deep within. After all, both nature and the divine are within me. I do not exist in a bubble set apart from the rest of the universe.

If we are to make the world a better place in which to live – the primary object of civilization – then we must come to terms with what the world really is. This is easier said than done, of course, for there is no aspect of the world about which we all agree. Despite this, I do think it is possible for humankind as a whole to reach a basic understanding of the natural world – an understanding predicated by the uncertainty that hounds us all. And when that day comes, when reality becomes more precious to us than the words we use to describe it, we will all be pantheists to some greater or lesser extent. Then we will flourish in the divine.

Epilogue: Eternal Renewal

After a long cold winter, there isn't much I want more than to tramp across bare ground, laying boot tracks in half-frozen mud. I'm not one of those people who glide gleefully down mountain slopes on skis, immersed in the clean pleasure of Vermont's winter wonderland. Instead I spend the darker months of the year indoors, as dormant as the rest of nature, lost in my thoughts until the snow melts and the migrating birds return. Oh sure, I own a pair of snowshoes, and I use them to escape cabin fever late in the cold season. But it is the feel of raw earth underfoot that I long for, accompanied by the first signs of nature's reawakening. So when the woods in the Champlain Valley shed their snowy coat, I tell my dog Matika to get into the car. Then I drive to a nearby trailhead.

I leave my car in the empty parking lot at Niquette Bay State Park then amble down the trail. Matika leaps ahead until she comes to the first interesting smell. A few patches of snow still linger in the deep ravines and beneath conifers. I ignore them. Instead I focus on the rivulets of snowmelt making their way down to the still frozen lake. Half-eaten cones are scattered along the trail.   Squirrels scurry about, keeping my canine companion busy. I quickly break a sweat beneath the wools and thermals that I'm wearing. Still unsure of the season, I am overdressed. I won't shed these layers until the first wildflowers come up. That's still weeks away.

The surrounding forest is dull brown for the most part, though a few ferns and moss-covered rocks sport last year's green. My eyes hunger for the color that indicates growth, so I read more into the ferns than I should. Then I caress the moss, assuring myself that it is real, that its green-ness isn't a figment of my imagination. That's what a long winter of abstract thought does to me. It turns me into a doubting Thomas. By early spring, I believe only what I can touch.

After a long cold winter, the forest is a grim place. Often I find the bleached bones of creatures that didn't make it. The trees themselves show the wear and tear of the season. Some of them are on the ground – a woody buffet laid before a host of insects, fungus, and other opportunists. Overhead a woodpecker pecks at a half-dead tree still standing, making a meal out of insects that haven't risen from their winter slumber yet. All nature is opportunistic it seems. All nature is the interplay of growth and decay. This is especially apparent in springtime, when the first wild lily pushes up through the skull of a fallen deer.

Last fall I knelt before the fossilized remnants of creatures that lived hundreds of millions of years ago. Now I wander through a world where death is more recent, thereby making life seem that much more precious. As I follow in the footsteps of my previous self, hiking a trail that I've hiked many times before, I sense my own mortality. I'm a little older now than I was the last time I was here, and not as agile as I used to be. In time, I too will fall to the ground as the greatest trees do, becoming food for those still living. That's a sobering thought. Then I look around at the trees still standing, fully aware that time means nothing to the forest. Trees die, but the forest lives on. So it is with all nature. Flora and fauna die, but nature lives on. And there it is, the essence of a pantheistic worldview.

Nature with a capital "N" lives on. The natural world shouts this message every moment of every day. In early spring even the most thickheaded among us can hear it, see it, even smell it. Eternal renewal – that's what springtime and the symbols associated with it are all about. Nature lives on. Individuals come and go, but the One is forever. Call it whatever you want: God, Being, Logos, Tao, the Absolute, whatever. The One is forever. Mystics of every stripe know this. The natural world is all growth and decay. The elements take on an infinite variety of forms, constantly changing, morphing from one thing into another. It is the incredibly complex dance of order and chaos, resisting any simplistic explanation of things. It is a report rendered to us through our senses, boggling our minds, making mincemeat of what we'd like to think the world is all about.

Despite what we believe, despite everything that we hold to be true, nature lives on. *Why?* Every philosophy and religion is an attempt to answer this question. Yet the basis of all our worldviews is nothing more than the impression the wild makes upon us during any given outing in early spring. All our religious/philosophical interpretations of it are only smoke, guesswork, speculation. Nature reveals itself to me in a mystical moment and suddenly I think I know what is real. But when I try to articulate it, I become tongue-tied. Something is always lost in translation. Truth is, no one knows the mind of God. No one knows anything more about the Absolute than the next person. It goes beyond words, beyond knowing.

And yet the natural world is as real as we are. More to the point, there is nothing super-natural, nothing beyond nature – not even us. Reason exists within nature. Everything reported by our senses is within nature. The entire universe and everything in it is within nature. Even God is within nature, because the word "nature" is meaningless without some kind of organizing force backing it up. At some point, our understanding or lack thereof becomes a matter of semantics. Language breaks down on the frontier of knowledge. All godtalk and the secular alternatives to it degenerate to babble in the face of reality. Then we have Nature and only Nature, which is the first and last word on the subject. Everything else is speculation.

I wonder as I wander through the wild, then I write down what I imagine are my profound observations on the subject. But it is all smoke. During the first hike of the spring season, the stark reality of the natural world humbles me. If I am honest with myself, that is. It made a fool of me when I was teenage seeker, when I was a full-grown man immersed in the Alaskan bush, and on many other occasions. Now, as gray-haired fellow tramping the cold mud of early April, I feel the full weight of Nature. During my outings, I witness firsthand the eternal renewal about which I have no control or complete understanding. Then I speculate as my distant ancestors speculated, filling in the gaps where there are no facts, making sense of the world however I can. Like them, I look beyond the frontier of knowledge and see God. What else could I see? "God" is the only word that adequately describes what I cannot possibly grasp, or should that word be "Nature"? To wanderers like me, it is one and the same.

Notes

Quote Page

"Most people..." Henry David Thoreau, *A Week on the Concord and Merrimack Rivers* (Holt, Rinehart & Winston, 1963), p. 54.

Chapter 1 - Godtalk

"Among the non-human primates..." Grahame Clark, *Space, Time and Man: A Prehistorian's View* (Cambridge University Press, 1994), p.39.

"When people first began to ask..." *Space, Time and Man: A Prehistorian's View*, p. 40.

"The word God..." Ursula Goodenough, *The Sacred Depths of Nature* (Oxford University Press, 1998), p. 11.

"The man of the archaic societies..." Mircea Eliade, *The Sacred and the Profane* (Harcourt, Brace & World, 1959), p. 12.

"A purely rational man..." *The Sacred and the Profane*, p. 209

Chapter 2 – The Ultimate Question

"We exist..." William Barrett, *Death of the Soul: From Descartes to the Computer* (Anchor Press/Doubleday, 1987), p. 87.

"But this trouble..." St. John of the Cross, *Dark Night of the Soul* (Image Books/ Doubleday, 1959), third revised edition, p. 70.

"The longest silence..." *The Journal of Henry David Thoreau*, edited by Bradford Torrey and Francis H. Allen (Gibbs M. Smith, 1984), volume 2, p. 137.

Chapter 3 – Reason and Revelation

"He thinks that he knows..." Socrates as presented by Plato in *The Last Days of Socrates* (Penguin Books, 1980 reprint), p. 50.

"Everywhere in the sixth century..." George Woodcock, *The Marvellous Century: Archaic Man and the Awakening of Reason* (Black Rose Books, 2006), p. 6.

"Direct experience is the foundation..." Pandit Rajmani Tigunait, *Seven Systems of Indian Philosophy* (The Himalayan International Institute of Yoga Science and Philosophy of the USA, 1998), fifth printing, p. 21.

"The Upanishads unanimously maintain..." *Seven Systems of Indian Philosophy*, p. 215.

"Such is the scope of the All-pervading Power..." Taken from the *Tao Te Ching,* written by Lao Tzu*,* found in Arthur Waley's book, *The Way and Its Power* (Grove Press, 1958), thirteenth printing, p. 170.

"There was something formless..." *Tao Te Ching*, found in *The Way and Its Power*, p. 174.

"Tao gave birth to the One..." *Tao Te Ching*, found in *The Way and Its Power*, p. 195.

"If faith is understood..." Paul Tillich, *Dynamics of Faith* (Harper & Row, 1958), p. 18.

"Is there a courage..." Paul Tillich, *The Courage to Be* (Yale University Press, 1961), fifth printing, p. 174-75.

"For those who enter..." Martin Buber, *I and Thou* (Charles Scribner's Sons, 1970), p. 127.

"This is the sublime melancholy..." *I and Thou*, p. 68.

Chapter 4 – Spiritual Wandering

"A joyous apprehension of the Absolute." Evelyn Underhill, *Mysticism* (New American Library, 1974), p. 240.

"Certain aspects of nature..." William James, *The Varieties of Religious Experience* (Random House, 1902), Modern Library edition, p. 384-86.

"To wage war against despair unceasingly." Thomas Merton, *Thoughts in Solitude* (Doubleday, 1968), Image books edition, p. 23.

"When you go deep..." Part of a poem by Hsieh Ling-yun, taken from the anthology *Mountain Home: The Wilderness Poetry of Ancient China*, translated by David Hinton (New Directions, 2005), p. 29.

"The infinite bustle of Nature..." *The Journal of Henry David Thoreau*, volume 1, p. 133.

"I do not prefer one religion or philosophy..." *The Journal of Henry David Thoreau*, volume 2, p. 4.

Chapter 5 – The Cult of Alders

"It is in solitude..." Sam Campbell, *Nature's Messages: A Book of Wilderness Wisdom* (Rand McNally, 1952), p. 155.

"The solitary is a man who has made a decision..." *Thoughts in Solitude*, p. 97.

"I am a part of the whole..." Taken from *The Meditations of Marcus Aurelius,* translated by George Long (Doubleday, 1963), a Dolphin reprint, p. 110.

Chapter 6 – God's Nature

"If God were not in everything..." *Meister Eckhart: A Modern Translation* by Raymond B. Blakney (Harper & Row, 1986 reprint), p. 168.

"It is by The One that all beings are beings." Plotinus, *Enneads,* excerpted in *The Essential Plotinus*, translated by Elmer O'Brien (New American Library, 1964), p. 73.

"The One is without form..." *The Essential Plotinus*, p. 77.

The One is not a being..." *The Essential Plotinus*, p 77.

"When we are told that God made anything..." Taken from John Scotus Erigena's book, *The Division of Nature*, which is excerpted in *Medieval Philosophy*, edited by Herman Shapiro (Random House, 1964), Modern Library edition, p. 96.

"In Erigena's paradoxical theology, God is both Everything and Nothing." Karen Armstrong, *A History of God* (Ballantine Books, 1994), p. 199.

"The Faylasufs were attempting..." *A History of God*, p. 172.

"God is a Necessary Being..." *Avicenna on Theology*, translated by A. J. Arberry (Kazi Publications, 2007), p. 32.

"Of God himself can no man think..." *The Cloud of Unknowing and Other Works*, translated into modern English by Clifton Wolters (Penguin Books, 1978), p. 67.

"It is God's nature to be without a nature." *Meister Eckhart: A Modern Translation*, p. 243.

Chapter 7 – Natural Theology

"Thus is the excellence of God magnified..." Giordano Bruno, *On the Infinite Universe and Worlds*, excerpted in *Theories of the World from Antiquity to the Copernican Revolution*, by Michael J. Crowe (Dover, 2001), second edition, p. 174.

"My book, O philosopher, is the nature of created things..." The reply of St. Anthony in to a query by an unnamed philosopher in *The Wisdom of the Desert*, translated by Thomas Merton (New Directions, 1970), p. 62.

"Nature is an infinite sphere..." Blaise Pascal, *Pensées*, translated by A. J. Krailsheimer (Penguin Books, 1979 reprint), p. 89.

"The use of reason is not so dangerous..." John Toland, *Christianity Not Mysterious*, excerpted in *Deism and Natural Religion*, edited by E. Graham Waring (Frederick Ungar Publishing, 1967), p. 1.

"I assert that what is once revealed..." *Christianity Not Mysterious*, excerpted in *Deism and Natural Religion*, p. 25.

"I regard it as the irresistible effect..." Quoted from a sermon that Ralph Waldo Emerson gave in May, 1832, found in *Emerson: The Mind on Fire*, by Robert D. Richardson Jr. (University of California Press, 1995), p. 124.

"The foregoing generations beheld God..." Ralph Waldo Emerson, *Nature* (Beacon Press, 1989), facsimile of the first edition, p. 5.

"In the woods we return..." *Nature*, p. 12-13.

"All things proceed out of the same spirit..." Taken from Emerson's address at the Harvard Divinity School in July 1838, reprinted in *The Complete Essays and Other Writings of Ralph Waldo Emerson*, edited by Brooks Atkinson (Random House, 1950), p. 69-70.

"To go alone; to refuse all good models…" *The Complete Essays and Other Writings of Ralph Waldo Emerson*, p. 81.

"He was a pantheist…" What the literary historian Van Wyck Brooks actually wrote in *The Flowering of New England 1815-1865* was: "The Cambridge theologians reviled him: he was a pantheist and a German mystic, and his style was a kind of neo-Platonic moonshine." (Dutton, 1937), p. 196.

Chapter 8 – Belief and Unbelief

"It is the opium of the people." Written by Karl Marx in a paper called "A Contribution to the Critique of Hegel's Philosophy of Right," first published in Deutsch-Französische Jahrbücher in 1844. A transcript of it in English can be found at https://www.marxists.org/archive/marx/works/1843/critique-hpr/intro.htm.

"But religion appears…" Arthur Schopenhauer, *Religion: A Dialogue and Other Essays* (Books for Libraries Press, 1972), p. 50.

"The error of imaginary causes…" Friedrich Nietzsche, *Twilight of the Idols & The Anti-Christ*, translated by R. J. Hollingdale (Penguin Books, 1975 reprint), p. 50.

"We deny God…" *Twilight of the Idols & The Anti-Christ*, p. 54.

"I doubt if any mind…" John Burroughs, *The Light of Day,* volume XI of *The Writings of John Burroughs* (Houghton Mifflin, 1904), p. 183.

"The claim that God is the creator…" Michael P. Levine, *Pantheism: A Non-theistic Concept of Diety* (Routledge, 2014), first paperback edition, p. 152.

"Ontology is a messy business." *Pantheism: A Non-theistic Concept of Diety,* p. 153.

Chapter 9 – God and the Cosmos

"The multiverse..." Richard Dawkins, *The God Delusion* (Houghton Mifflin, 2008), p. 174.

"The anthropic principle..." *The God Delusion*, p. 164.

"Some collapsing phase of the universe..." Roger Penrose, *Cycles of Time: An Extraordinary New View of the Universe* (Alfred Knopf, 2011), p. 143.

"Finds that these fundamental laws..." Albert Einstein quoted by Sir James Jeans in *Physics and Philosophy* (Dover, 1981 reprint), p. 183.

"Our conclusion must be..." Paul Davies, *God and the New Physics*, (Simon & Schuster, 1984), p. 186.

"How does a collection of molecules..." Neil deGrasse Tyson and Donald Goldsmith, *Origins: Fourteen Billion Years of Cosmic Evolution* (Norton, 2005), p. 243.

"The universe endures..." Henri Bergson, *Creative Evolution* (Dover, 1998), p. 11.

"To the intelligent..." A short essay called "Nature" in *Emerson's Essays*, not to be confused with the book by the same name (Thomas Crowell, 1961), Apollo reprint, p. 399.

Chapter 10 – The God of Wildness

"One must always cross-question nature..." Taken from the essay "A Sharp Lookout," by John Burroughs, *Signs and Seasons* (Harper & Row, 1981), p. 14.

"How natural is 'natural'..." Loren Eiseley, *The Firmament of Time* (Univ. of Nebraska Press, 1999), p. 157.

"Nature, the sum of its laws…" Abraham J. Heschel, *Who is Man?* (Stanford Univ. Press, 1965), p. 91.

"Our studies can never…" *Physics and Philosophy*, p. 16.

"Becoming is infinitely varied." *Creative Evolution*, p. 304.

"Nature… everywhere presents disorder…" *Creative Evolution*, p. 40.

"Any God with whom facts could conflict…" Charles Hartshorne, *A Natural Theology for Our Time* (Open Court, 1973), second printing, p. 79

"The only 'acts of God'…" *A Natural Theology for Our Time*, p. 102

Chapter 11 – The Pantheistic Worldview

"Modern Pantheism as a religion…" J. Allanson Picton, *Pantheism: Its Story and Significance* (Forgotten Books, 2013 reprint) p. 56.

"By God, I mean…" Benedict de Spinoza, *The Ethics*, reprinted in *The Rationalists* (Doubleday/Anchor Books, 1974), p. 179.

"Whatever is, is in God…" *The Ethics*, reprinted in *The Rationalists*, p. 189.

"The pantheist claims…" Michael P. Levine, *Pantheism: A Non-theistic Concept of Diety* (Routledge, 2014), first paperback edition, p. 191.

"For the pantheist…" *Pantheism: A Non-theistic Concept of Diety*, p. 28.

"In the view of Pantheism…" *Pantheism: Its Story and Significance,* p. 9.

"Pantheism is sexed-up atheism." Richard Dawkins, *The God Delusion* (Houghton Mifflin, 2008), p. 40.

"Pantheists don't believe…" *The God Delusion*, p. 39-40.

"The precise opposite of Atheism…" *Pantheism: Its Story and Significance,* p. 10.

"There never has been a pantheistic church…" *Pantheism: A Non-theistic Concept of Diety,* p. 358.

Chapter 12 – The Grand Scheme of Things

"We see the world…" From a short essay called "The Over-Soul" in *Emerson's Essays* (Thomas Crowell, 1961), p. 190.

"His infinite simplicity…" Thomas Merton, *Seeds of Contemplation* (New Directions, 1949), p.13.

"God's glory fills the whole earth…" Taken from *The Wisdom of the Jewish Mystics*, translated by Alan Unterman (New Directions, 1976), p. 77.

"The Necessary Being cannot be two…" *Avicenna on Theology*, p. 26.

"God is in truth the whole universe…" *The Upanishads,* translated by Juan Mascaró (Penguin Books, 1965), p. 90.

"Great knowledge sees all…" *The Way of Chuang Tzu*, edited by Thomas Merton (New Directions, 1969,) p. 40.

"The chief objection I have…" Arthur Schopenhauer, *Religion: A Dialogue and Other Essays* (Books for Libraries Press, 1972), p. 55.

"The Great Way is not named." *Chuang Tzu: Basic Writings*, translated by Burton Watson (Columbia University Press, 1964) p. 39.

"Theism claims God is transcendent…" *Pantheism: A Non-theistic Concept of Diety*, p. 2.

"Nature is very complex indeed…" *A Natural Theology for Our Time*, p. 99.

Chapter 13 – A Reluctant Pantheism

"The eye with which you look…" Soren Kierkegaard, *Either/Or, Volume I* (Princeton Univ. Press, 1971), first paperback edition, p. 296.

"Nature loves to hide." Chet Raymo quoting Heraclitus, *When God is Gone, Everything is Holy* (Sorin Books, 2008), p. 15.

"Our response to the natural world…" *When God is Gone, Everything is Holy,* p. 104.

"I don't know whether this world has a meaning…" Albert Camus, *The Myth of Sisyphus and Other Essays* (Random House, 1955), p. 38.

"If we are to arrive at what exists…" Paul Weiss, *Being and Other Realities* (Open Court, 1995), p. 185.

"The mass of mankind are not yet prepared…" John Burroughs, *The Light of Day,* volume XI of *The Writings of John Burroughs* (Houghton Mifflin, 1904), p. 78.

"Man's quest for certainty…" Loren Eiseley, *The Firmament of Time* (University of Nebraska Press, 1999), p. 179.

"Pantheism has its roots in Mysticism." W. T. Stace, *Mysticism and Philosophy* (Jeremy P. Tarcher, 1987 reprint), p. 212.

"This is the glorious paradox of our existence…" Martin Buber, *Pointing the Way* (Harper and Brothers, 1957), p. 27.

About the Author

Walt McLaughlin received a degree in philosophy from Ohio University in 1977 and has been wondering, wandering and writing ever since. He has a dozen books in print, including a narrative about his immersion in the Alaskan bush, *Arguing with the Wind*, and one about backpacking through the Adirondacks, *The Allure of Deep Woods*. He is also the force behind a small press called Wood Thrush Books, and has selected and published the works of several 19th Century writers including *The Laws of Nature: Excerpts from the Writings of Ralph Waldo Emerson*. He lives in Swanton, Vermont with his wife, Judy.

For more information about Walt's books, visit the WTB website: **www.woodthrushbooks.com**

Go to **www.facebook.com\WaltMcLaughlin** to check out his Facebook page, or read his regularly posted blogs at **www.woodswanderer.com**

89014960R00088

Made in the USA
Columbia, SC
15 February 2018